Don't Be Worried About Unappetizing Salt-free Foods!

By substituting herbs, spices, and wine you will discover that a whole new taste dimension is opened by a salt-restricted diet. Many people who stop using salt later find an occasional salted restaurant dinner to be extremely unpalatable after the joys of cooking with herbs and spices.

Just be creative and try different ingredients from time to time. You'll find you enjoy eating more as you improve your health!

SHAKE THE SALT HABIT!

The Salt Content Guide for
Food, Beverages, and Medicines

DR. KERMIT R. TANTUM

BALLANTINE BOOKS • NEW YORK

ISBN 0-345-30183-8

This edition published by arrangement with
Gabriel Books

Manufactured in the United States of America

First Ballantine Books Edition: November 1982

For
Jeff, Greg and John

CONTENTS

FOREWORD

Supermarket and restaurant food in America contains shocking amounts of salt!

Excessive salt is added to canned vegetables, fruit, and soups, to many frozen vegetables, to ice cream, cheese, bouillon cubes, TV and specialty dinners, pizza, candy, salads, cereals, crackers, bread, and nearly all baked goods!

Some foods, including hot dogs, ham, and bacon require the addition of salt to prevent spoilage. Unfortunately, the amount of salt added to these meats is far in excess of that needed for safety. In short, there is salt in virtually every processed food on supermarket shelves. The problem is, no one can tell how much salt is added to foods because labels seldom specify the amount actually used.

Table salt, or sodium chloride, is about forty per cent sodium. The average American consumes five to fifteen grams of salt every day! The normal requirement is only a fraction of that. And the desire for this taste is learned, not natural. We learn to love salt very early because many baby foods are very heavily salted. Processed meats can have six times more salt than natural meats, cereals are loaded with one hundred times more salt, and processed vegetables routinely carry six to sixty times more salt than those picked from the garden. When you consider that dairy milk contains six hundred times as much salt as found in a mother's natural milk, is it any wonder that we're hooked on salt for life before we're ready to crawl?

Many consumers may not realize that salt also is present in monosodium glutamate, sodium nitrite, sodium benzoate, and other additives beginning with sodium. In addition, the water supplies of many cities contain abnormally high amounts of sodium, as does any household water treated by softeners. And road salt, often used to an inexcusable extent, is finding its way into the water supplies of many communities!

Too much salt in the diet can be extremely dangerous! It can lead to high blood pressure (hypertension), heart disease, stroke, premenstrual anxiety and tension in women, kidney problems, and other maladies. One in every five Americans, twenty-five million in all, is a victim of high blood pressure. Many more are suspected of having hypertension, but, because so few are tested, accurate statistics are impossible. Hypertension's symptoms may present with chest pains, shortness of breath, headaches, and heart palpitations. But for many people living with hypertension, their first sign of the disease may be a heart attack, stroke, or kidney failure!

High blood pressure is extremely rare in societies where people consume less than four grams of salt per day. These societies keep stable blood pressure all their lives. But in America, blood pressure routinely rises as we grow older. Many studies have proved the link between salt intake and high blood pressure, showing that patients with hypertension can be treated successfully by restricting salt, fats, and cholesterol in the diet. However, during the 1950's, drugs to combat hypertension were developed. It soon became routine practice for physicians to prescribe diuretics and other drugs for their patients to take every day. Not only are these drugs expensive, but also many patients use them reluctantly because of noxious side effects. Some of these drugs can cause drowsiness, ulcers, mental depression, and repressed sex drive, so patients understandably may stop using the drugs without informing their physicians.

A far more practicable method of fighting high blood pressure is to reduce salt intake. The human body needs very little salt. Our primitive ancestors probably consumed about six hundred milligrams —six-tenths of one gram—of sodium each day.

Craig Claiborne and other great chefs have written about enjoying a long life on a salt-free diet. They advocate the use of condiments, herbs, and spices, especially pepper, as superior replacements for salt.

Craig Claiborne and Pierre Franey authored a Gourmet Diet Cookbook based on a salt-free regimen and soon lost twenty pounds following their own advice. Before going on a salt-free diet, Craig Claiborne suffered from edema (water retention) and a seemingly unquenchable thirst that would awaken him repeatedly throughout the night. After starting a salt-free diet, edema and excessive thirst disappeared. And his blood pressure dropped from 186 over 112 to a normal reading of 140 over 80!

Many other victims of high blood pressure have shown similar results on a reduced or salt-free diet. To help others enjoy the benefits possible from a salt-restricted life style, SHAKE THE SALT HABIT provides comprehensive listings of foods, beverages, and many medicines, showing the weight and sodium content of each specific item.

By using SHAKE THE SALT HABIT, many victims of high blood pressure will have the opportunity to painlessly correct their condition. And many others, who would have developed hypertension, can altogether avoid the disease!

INTRODUCTION

Salt and Health

Salt or sodium chloride is essential to our life and well being. Every cell in our body is bathed in a salt and water environment and can only live, grow, and function so long as this environment is kept constant. Why then do we read and hear with increasing frequency that we should reduce our salt intake, and that salt can be dangerous to our health? How can this vital life substance play a role in such serious medical problems as hypertension, stroke, heart attack, and kidney disease. The answer can in large part be attributed to the "civilized" diet of modern man, with its clearly excessive salt content. While other factors such as stress, obesity, heredity, and a sedentary life certainly play a role, it is now abundantly clear that excessive intake of salt is a major contributor to these disease processes and a major health hazard to a large proportion of our population. Most physicians and nutritionists would agree that a prudent diet should include far less than the 10 grams (approximately 2 teaspoons) of daily salt intake (4,000 milligrams of sodium) the average American eats. There is almost uniform agreement that this intake level becomes especially critical in those persons with most forms of hypertension. From my perspective as a physician and the medical director of a critical care complex I see all too often the extreme physical, emotional, and financial toll of these disease processes as they reach their final stages.

It is probable that in the near future the tables found in this book will no longer be necessary. Food manufacturers will in all likelihood be required to label food stuffs with the quantity of salt in their products. Until such time arrives it is hoped that the information contained herein will assist those persons who wish to reduce their daily dietary intake of salt. As further background to understanding and using these tables the following is a brief description of current medical thinking about salt and its role in health and disease.

Salt and Body Fluid

Approximately 60% of the body mass of an average adult is water. This means that the body of a person weighing 70 kilograms contains 40 liters of water. This fluid is divided into that which is located within the cells of the body called intracellular fluid, and that located outside of the cells called extracellular fluid (ECF). The total of 40 liters is divided approximately as follows: 25 liters within the cells and 15 liters outside the cells. The extracellular fluid is further divided into two compartments. That which is found within the blood vessels of the body (approximately ⅓ and called the intravascular volume) and that outside of the blood vessels bathing each and every cell of the body (approximately ⅔ and called the interstitial volume). It is this extracellular (intravascular plus interstitial) fluid volume that is of particular interest with respect to salt. Extracellular fluid is rich in both sodium and chloride, the two components of common salt. Of extreme importance is the fact that it is the amount of sodium in this extracellular fluid that determines its volume which in turn is a critical factor

.in controlling blood pressure. There are of course many other substances in this extracellular fluid important to life, including oxygen, and fuels such as glucose, amino acids, and fatty substances. The entire extracellular fluid volume of our body is in constant motion and is rapidly mixed, first by the blood circulation and secondly by a process called diffusion which occurs across the tiny blood vessels called capillaries. Diffusion thus links the two portions of the ECF volume, the intravascular and the interstitial compartments. As a result of this constant motion of fluid, all cells of our body live in an identical environment. This constancy has given rise to the term "milieu interieur" or internal environment.

Physiologists use the term "homeostasis" to describe remarkably complex systems of the body which function to maintain this constant internal environment. These systems, often called control systems, number in the thousands and function not unlike a thermostat which controls the temperature in your home. An example of one control system would be: a rise in the blood level of carbon dioxide (which might result from vigorous exercise) is sensed by the brain, this in turn sends out a signal to the muscles of our breathing apparatus to increase our ventilation and thereby lower the carbon dioxide level. Of particular importance to this discussion is the control system which regulates both the concentration of sodium and the volume of the extracellular fluid.

How does our body maintain the constant sodium concentration and volume of its extracellular fluid? It does so by striking a balance between the intake and output of salt and water and to do this there are control systems for both intake and output. In part the volume of water that we drink depends on habit, but more importantly it depends upon the amount of salt that we ingest. The ingested salt which is absorbed into our bloodstream is detected by a thirst center located in our brain which in turn stimulates us to drink water. As far as salt intake is concerned, it is well known that a person depleted of salt will crave this substance. This craving is obviously another homeostatic mechanism attempting to normalize body function. It should be noted that a deficiency of salt under most circumstances occurs only if salt intake falls below 500 mgm/day (1/20 of the average person's intake). It appears, however, that our control mechanism for salt intake is geared only towards dealing with deficiencies and not excesses of salt, i.e., excess ingestion does not result in less desire to eat salt. In fact, excessive voluntary use of salt is probably nothing more than habit. Thus, we have the dilemma of modern man with his processed foods containing large quantities of salt and his ever present salt shaker, ingesting far more than is needed for bodily function.

How do we rid ourselves of this excessive intake of salt and therefore water? The answer is by controlling the output of these substances. In fact the normal healthy human has great reserve to rid the body of excess fluid and salt, so that our extracellular volume and sodium concentration change very little despite wide variations of intake of these substances. The primary organ which is responsible for the output and therefore regulation of salt and water is the kidney. The schema which involves several control systems and regulates the volume and concentration of sodium in our extracellular fluid volume is as follows:

1) Intake of excessive salt and water
2) Causes an increase in extracellular volume

3) This causes the heart to pump more vigorously
4) This raises the blood pressure
5) The raised blood pressure signals our kidney to increase its urine formation resulting in water and sodium excretion.

A reduced intake of salt and water would have exactly the opposite effect. It is this "kidney-blood volume-pressure" control system which regulates the balance betweeen intake and output of salt and water and its proper function is essential to arterial blood pressure control.

Blood Pressure, Hypertension, and Its Effects

Blood pressure is the result of the blood being pumped by our heart meeting the resistance of the branching system of blood vessels in our body. The regulation of blood pressure within a fairly constant range is important in supplying local blood flow which in turn supplies nutrients to the various organs and tissues of our bodies. Normal blood pressure varies at different stages of our lives. The table below is the range of values from the newborn through an 80 year old. The systolic and diastolic pressures represent the high and low pressure points for each heart beat.

Age (years)	0	20	40	60	80
Pressure mm Hg					
systolic	90 /	110 /	125 /	140 /	160 /
diastolic	/ 50	/ 70	/ 80	/ 85	/ 85

Our bodies utilize numerous control mechanisms, some of which are short term systems and others long term systems, to maintain a normal blood pressure. An example of a short term system would be the adjustment of blood pressure as made when we stand up from a lying position. The fall in blood pressure which often occurs is immediately sensed and a constriction of blood vessels results, thus avoiding a loss of blood flow to the head and possible fainting. As mentioned previously, the most important factor in long term control or regulation of blood pressure is through the kidney-blood volume-pressure control system.

Hypertension is an exceedingly common medical problem which is diagnosed by the measurement of a blood pressure significantly in excess of the normal figures. For many years it has been generally agreed that the most important number is the diastolic blood pressure, and that a figure greater than 95 millimeters of mercury represents hypertension. It is now felt that in certain groups, i.e., men below the age of 45, a diastolic pressure of greater than 90 mm Hg may represent hypertension. Certainly a diastolic pressure above 105 mm Hg is considered to be significant hypertension. Recently more attention has been paid to the systolic pressure and its role in disease processes as well.

It is estimated that between 15 and 30% of the adults in the United States have hypertension. A large number of this group have no symptoms, are undetected, and are therefore untreated.

In over 90% of individuals with hypertension the cause of the disease is unknown, hence the term essential or primary hypertension. The remaining 6 to 8% of persons with hypertension are said to have secondary hypertension. This means that there is a known and usually correctable cause for the high blood pressure. Examples of secondary hypertension would include: an obstruction to the artery which supplies the kidneys and the excessive production of hormones which are capable of raising blood pressure.

INTRODUCTION

There is a growing body of evidence that the kidneys play a central role in most forms of hypertension. Of particular importance to this discussion is an alteration in the kidney which requires an elevated blood pressure for the organ to eliminate salt and water. It now appears that many persons do not have the normal feedback mechanism wherein a rise in blood pressure results in an appropriate output of salt and water. These persons have been described as salt sensitive or volume sensitive individuals.

While a normal person can increase his salt intake many fold and excrete this with minimal change in blood pressure, the salt sensitive individual can only handle increased intake of salt by raising his blood pressure. On the other hand, salt sensitive individuals can handle a low intake of salt with ease but alas as his intake rises so must his blood pressure. It must be emphasized that hypertension is an extremely complex disease process and certainly it is not simply a result of too much salt ingestion or too little elimination. It is well known that there are many hormonal, nervous, and other mechanisms at work in most types of hypertension. There is, however, a growing body of evidence that a change in this "renal output" function is a fundamental process in hypertension.

When hypertension is untreated it is now documented that there is a shortening of life of between 10 and 20 years. Usually this shortened life span is a result of a disease process called atherosclerosis which affects the arteries of the body. It is this process of atherosclerosis which can result in stroke, heart attack, and serious kidney disease. Hypertension is thus a major public health problem which is usually asymptomatic in its early stages, and often lethal if left untreated.

Evidence For a Causal Relationship Between Salt and Hypertension

Much of the information we have that relates salt intake to hypertension comes from studies conducted on populations in many parts of the world. Of considerable interest have been whole societies in which blood pressure remains low throughout life and hypertension is rare or absent. Over 20 of these low blood pressure populations have been described representing different races, diets, and climates. Included in these groups are Micronesians, Eskimos, Melanesians, Polynesians, Easter Islanders, several different African groups, and populations from Central and South America. Great diversity has been found among these populations. Their habitat varies from arctic to jungle to desert. Their diets vary widely including hunters who live on berries and game, others who exist largely on coconut and fish, and still others largely carnivorous. What emerges after carefully studying these populations for factors that might contribute to hypertension is that all of these populations habitually use diets which are *low* in *sodium*. Virtually all low blood pressure populations have a salt intake below 4 grams per day. One could conclude that these populations are simply not susceptable to hypertension. Such is not the case, for when members of these populations change to a more Westernized diet, hypertension ensues. An example of this was found in a group of men from Samburu, who were drafted into the army in Kenya. When their diet was changed from the civilian one containing less than 3 grams of salt to the army diet containing 15 grams per day, their blood pressure began to rise. This rise was seen during their second year in the army and continued to rise thru the sixth year. On the other extreme there are other populations that habitually ingest extremely high amounts of salt, greater than 17 grams per day. Examples are certain groups from Japan and Korea. Among these populations there is a very high prevalence of hypertension and stroke. In populations where there is an intermediate intake of salt, such as the United States, the incidence of hypertension is also at an intermediate level. It must be emphasized that not all members of a population group develop hypertension when their diet contains large amounts of salt.

A great deal of experimental work has been done with rats relating salt ingestion and blood pressure. Much of this work has been done by Louis K. Dahl who, as a part of his life long interest in dietary salt, developed and experimented with two very special strains of rats. One strain was exquisitely susceptible to salt induced hypertension and the other highly resistant to it. Of great interest was an experiment with these animals in which he transplanted the kidneys from a sensitive animal to a resistant one, following which the blood pressure of the resistant animal went up. These experiments clearly revealed a genetic basis for salt induced hypertension and further that the kidney carried the blood pressure message.

These population studies together with the animal experiments have led to the general conclusion that in humans there is a genetic predisposition found in many members of society (estimated 10-30%) which will result in hypertension when there is an excessive salt intake.

Further evidence for the role of salt in hypertension comes from the often dramatic improvement in blood pressure which occurs with the use of diuretics. Diuretics are drugs, often called "water pills," whose main function is to induce or force the kidney to excrete salt and water.

How Much Salt Should I Eat?

A safe and adequate salt intake for most persons is 3-4 grams (or 1,200-1,600 milligrams of sodium) per day. This represents a reduction in salt intake of approximately 60-70% in the typical American diet. While some authorities contend that an intake even lower than this is "optimal," this would be difficult for most persons in our society to achieve.

The following generalizations can be made:

1) Virtually no person will be harmed by lowering their intake to 3-4 grams per day (exceptions include persons subject to severe sweating or diarrhea and rare salt losing disease states).

2) A lowered salt intake may prevent or minimize hypertension in a large number of persons.

3) Most persons with established hypertension will benefit from salt intake reduction. Their antihypertensive medications will be more effective and possibly reduced in dosage as a result.

Until food manufacturers are required to label all foodstuffs, the amount of salt we take in (exclusive of the salt shaker) is a guessing game.

This book is intended as a guide to salt intake reduction for the healthy person, and as a supplement to expert medical management for those with known hypertension.

1. Arterial Pressure and Hypertension, Circulatory Physiology III, Arthur C. Guyton, MD, (Saunders) 1980.

INTRODUCTION

2. Hypertension: A Practical Approach, Marvin Moser, MD, 1975 (Little, Brown).
3. Hypertension Update: Mechanisms, Epidemiology, Evaluation, Management, James C. Hunt, MD, et al 1980. (H. L. S. Press). 1980.
4. Role of Hypertensions in Atherosclerosis and Cardiovascular Disease, Wm. Hollander, MD, The American Journal of Cardiology Vol. 38: 1976.
5. Salt and Hypertension, Lewis K. Dahl, MD, The American Journal of Clinical Nutrition, Vol 25, 1972.
6. Salt Shakes Up Some of Us, Louise Fenner, FDA Consumer, March 1980.
7. Salt, Volume and the Prevention of Hypertension, Edward D. Freis, MD, Circulation, Vol 53, April 1976.
8. Textbook of Medical Physiology, Arthur C. Guyton MD, Sixth Edition, (Saunders) 1981.

PREFACE

This book provides tables showing the sodium content of common foods (table 1) to help you determine how much sodium is in your diet. Table 2 lists the sodium content of selected non-prescription drugs.

In addition to the salt we knowingly sprinkle on our food (a teaspoon contains 5,000 milligrams), many foods contain sodium as a part of their normal chemical composition. Household staples like baking powder and baking soda are sodium compounds. Some popular flavoring agents high in sodium are soy sauce, worcestershire sauce, catsup, pickles, olives, garlic, onion, and celery salt.

Many processed foods contain added sodium. Salted or brined meats and fish are obviously higher in salt content than the uncured forms. Many canned vege-

tables are packed in a salt solution or
brine.

Frozen vegetables usually are processed
without added salt. However, starchy
vegetables like lima beans and peas frequently are sorted in brine before freez-
ing. Frozen vegetables with added sauces,
mushrooms, or nuts are higher in sodium than the plain varieties.

Canned and frozen fruits are not usually processed with added salt, but some
companies add small amounts of salt to
prevent darkening of some fruits and to
add to the flavor of applesauce and other
products. Some canned and frozen fruits,
and most canned whole tomatoes, are
dipped in sodium hydroxide so that they
can be easily peeled. This process causes
these foods to have higher sodium lev-
els than are found in the fresh foods.
Canned and bottled citrus drinks are
sometimes buffered with sodium citrate.
Sodium ion exchange is used in processing some wines to reduce sediment and
clarify the product.

Chemical ingredients which contain
sodium may be added during food processing. Some examples of these ingredients are monosodium glutamate or
MSG (a flavor enhancer); sodium sac-
charin (a sweetener); sodium phosphates

(emulsifiers, stablizers, buffers); sodium citrate (a buffer); sodium caseinate (a thickener and binder); and sodium nitrite (a preservative).

It is especially important for persons on salt-restricted diets to read ingredient labels carefully to see which, if any, sodium compounds have been included in processed foods. Those items listed first on the label are present in the largest amounts. Nutritional information on labels of some foods, such as breakfast cereals, shows sodium values. To allow for variability among packages, cereal manufacturers may show higher values on packages of cereal than those shown in the table.

Some over-the-counter drugs, particularly antacids, contain sodium in significant amounts. Read labels carefully and ask your physician about using such drugs. Refer to table 2 for a list of selected non-prescription drugs and the amount of sodium each contains.

Many patients with high blood pressure take diuretics and are advised to increase their potassium intake to replenish that lost in the increased urine volume. Bananas and orange juice are frequently recommended for their potassium content. Most fresh vegetables, fruits, legumes, and uncured meats are also good sources of potassium and add only small amounts of sodium to the diet. If you are thinking of using a potassium substitute for common salt, you should consult your physician before doing so.

Another source of sodium is drinking water. The sodium content of drinking water varies considerably throughout the country. This variation also affects the sodium content of soft drinks and beer produced and bottled at different locations.

Water softeners raise the sodium content of water—the harder the water, the greater amount of sodium needed to soften it. In most States, the State Department of Public Health can supply information on the sodium content of public water supplies and provide help in getting water from individual wells or water supplies analyzed.

Some food products vary considerably in sodium content, so table 1 in the following pages gives representative, or average, values of several different brands. The values were obtained from reports of laboratory analyses using flame photometry, atomic absorption, or emission spectroscopy to find the sodium content of foods, and were verified by the United

States Department of Agriculture. Sodium values shown reflect current processing practices and typical product formulas. If these practices and formulas are changed, sodium values may change also.

Values given in table 1 are for unsalted products, unless specified (Cooked items have been prepared using unsalted water, even though the manufacturers' instructions may call for salt). Canned vegetable values are for total can contents of solids and liquids. The values reported are for common household measures of the foods and include metric equivalents.

Some labels may express sodium content in grams or milligrams. Here's how to convert these measurements and also how to measure the amount of sodium in salt.

Salt and sodium conversions

Grams to
  milligrams ......Multiply weight in grams by 1,000

Sodium into
  salt (NaCl)
  equivalent ....Milligrams of sodium content ÷ .40 = milligrams of salt

Salt into sodium ... Milligrams of salt ×
.40 = milligrams
of sodium

Sodium in
milligrams to
sodium in milli-
equivalents[1] ..... Milligrams of
sodium ÷ 23
(atomic weight of
sodium) = milli-
equivalents of
sodium

Milliequivalents of
sodium to
milligrams of
sodium .... Milliequivalents of
sodium × 23 =
milligrams of
sodium

[1]Medical prescriptions are often given as milliequivalents (mEq).

TRY HERBS AND SPICES AND FORGET SALT FOREVER!

Don't be worried about unappetizing salt-free foods! By substituting herbs, spices, and wine you will discover that a whole new taste dimension is opened by a salt restricted diet. Many people who stop using salt later find an occasional salted restaurant dinner to be extremely unpalatable after the joys of cooking with herbs and spices. On the following pages you will find a list of recommended spices that complement individual dishes. But remember to be creative and try different ingredients from time to time! One of the great joys of cooking is the discovery of a new and exciting taste treat.

Try adding fresh lemon juice or a piece of lemon peel to cooking water. Lime may be used in the same way. Garlic and onions are excellent substitutes for salt. Diced garlic is a wonderful addition to meats like lamb, while freshly squeezed garlic juice adds zest to vegetables and salads. Raw or cooked onions, used in the same way as garlic, can make you forget that salt ever existed. Another excellent substitute for salt is pepper. Adding generous amounts of pepper to meats, soups, salads, vegetables, and other foods will enhance flavor, as will cooking with wine. In short there are innumerable ways to avoid using salt, and you will soon learn that cooking with herbs, spices, and wine will produce food with incomparably better taste!

The following is a list of suggested herbs and spices to add zest to any meal:

Food	Spice or herb
Asparagus	Mustard seed, sesame seed, or tarragon.
Beans, lima	Marjoram, oregano, sage, savory, tarragon, or thyme.
Beans, snap	Basil, dill, marjoram, mint, mustard seed, oregano, savory, or thyme.
Beef	Thyme, sage, marjoram, or bay leaf.

TRY HERBS AND SPICES

Food	Spice or herb
Beets	Allspice, bay leaves, caraway seed, cloves, dill, ginger, mustard seed, savory, or thyme.
Broccoli	Caraway seed, dill, mustard seed, or tarragon.
Brussels sprouts	Basil, caraway seed, dill, mustard seed, sage, or thyme.
Cabbage	Caraway seed, celery seed, dill, mint, mustard seed, nutmeg, savory, or tarragon.
Carrots	Allspice, bay leaves, caraway seed, dill, fennel, ginger, mace, marjoram, mint, nutmeg, or thyme.
Cauliflower	Caraway seed, celery salt, dill, mace, or tarragon.
Cucumbers	Basil, dill, mint, or tarragon.
Eggplant	Marjoram or oregano.
Eggs	Parsley, paprika, or curry.

TRY HERBS AND SPICES

Food	Spice or herb
Fish	Paprika, marjoram, bay leaf, or curry.
Lamb	Garlic, rosemary, curry, or mint.
Onions	Caraway seed, mustard seed, nutmeg, oregano, sage, or thyme.
Peas	Basil, dill, marjoram, mint, oregano, poppy seed, rosemary, sage, or savory.
Potatoes	Basil, bay leaves, caraway seed, celery seed, dill, chives, mustard seed, oregano, poppy seed, or thyme.
Poultry	Parsley, sage, thyme, or paprika.
Salad greens	Basil, chives, dill, or tarragon.
Spinach	Basil, mace, marjoram, nutmeg, or oregano.
Squash	Allspice, basil, cinnamon, cloves, fennel, ginger, mustard seed, nutmeg, or rosemary.

TRY HERBS AND SPICES

Food	Spice or herb
Sweet potatoes	Allspice, cardamom, cinnamon, cloves, or nutmeg.
Tomatoes	Basil, bay leaves, celery seed, oregano, sage, sesame seed, tarragon, or thyme.
Veal	Ginger, oregano, marjoram, or bay leaf.

Pepper and parsley may be added to any of the above. Curry powder is good with creamed vegetables.

A BASIC LIST
OF HIGH-SODIUM FOODS

Anchovies
Artichokes
Bacon
Baking soda
Beet greens
Bouillon cubes
Brains
Buttermilk
Catsup
Canned tomato
  juice
Caviar
Celery
Celery salt
Chard
Chili sauce
Clams
Cod
Cold cereals
Cold meats
Corned beef

Crab
Dulse
Garlic salt
Ham
Herring
Kale
Kelp
Kidney
Lobster
Meat
  tenderizers
Mustard
Olives
Onion salt
Pastrami
Pickles
Potato chips
Pretzels
Relishes
Salmon
Salt pork

A BASIC LIST OF HIGH-SODIUM FOODS

Salted peanuts &
  nuts
Sardines
Sauerkraut
Sausages
Scallops
Self-rising flour

Shellfish
Shrimp
Soy sauce
Spinach
Tuna
Worcestershire
  sauce

A BASIC LIST
OF LOW-SODIUM FOODS

Apples
Apricots
Asparagus
Bananas
Barley
Blackberries
Blueberries
Brown rice
Cherries
Chicken
Coffee
Cucumber
Eggplant
Farina
Grapes
Green beans
Green peppers
Honey
Macaroni
Maple syrup
Margarine

Oatmeal
Onion
Orange juice
Peaches
Peanut oil
Pears
Peas
Pineapple
Plain spaghetti
Polished rice
Potatoes
Puffed wheat
Raspberries
Shredded wheat
Squash
Strawberries
Sugar
Sweet corn
Sweet potatoes
Tangerines
Tea

A BASIC LIST OF LOW-SODIUM FOODS

Tomatoes
Vinegar
Watermelon

Whole wheat flour
Zucchini

TABLE 1
SODIUM CONTENT OF
FOODS, BEVERAGES
AND FRUIT JUICES

Food	Portion	Weight gms	Sodium mgs
ALCOHOLIC:			
Beer	12 fl oz	360	25
Gin, rum, whisky	2 fl oz	60	1
Wine:			
Red:			
Domestic	4 fl oz	120	12
Imported	4 fl oz	120	6
Sherry	4 fl oz	120	14
White:			
Domestic	4 fl oz	120	19
Imported	4 fl oz	120	2
BREAKFAST DRINK, INSTANT:			
Grape	8 fl oz	240	0
Citrus fruits	8 fl oz	240	14
CARBONATED:			
Club soda	8 fl oz	240	39

BEVERAGES AND FRUIT JUICES

Food	Portion	Weight gms	Sodium mgs
Cola:			
Regular	8 fl oz	240	16
Low calorie	8 fl oz	240	21
Fruit flavored:			
Regular	8 fl oz	240	34
Low calorie	8 fl oz	240	46
Ginger ale	8 fl oz	240	13
Root beer	8 fl oz	240	24
COCOA MIX, WATER ADDED	8 fl oz	240	232
COFFEE:			
Brewed	8 fl oz	240	2
Instant:			
Regular	8 fl oz	240	1
Decaffeinated	8 fl oz	240	1
With chicory	8 fl oz	240	7
With flavorings	8 fl oz	240	124
Substitute	8 fl oz	240	3
FRUIT DRINKS, CANNED:			
Apple	8 fl oz	240	16
Cranberry juice cocktail	8 fl oz	240	4
Grape	8 fl oz	240	1
Lemonade	8 fl oz	240	60

BEVERAGES AND FRUIT JUICES

Food	Portion	Weight gms	Sodium mgs
Orange	8 fl oz	240	77
Pineapple- Grapefruit	8 fl oz	240	80

**FRUIT DRINKS, DEHYDRATED,
RECONSTITUTED:**
Sweetened:

Lemonade	8 fl oz	240	50
Orange	8 fl oz	240	35
Other fruit	8 fl oz	240	0
Unsweetened, all flavors	8 fl oz	240	0

FRUIT JUICES:

Apple cider or juice	1 cup	248	5
Apricot nectar	1 cup	251	9
Citrus: Grapefruit juice:			
Canned	1 cup	250	4
Frozen, diluted	1 cup	247	5
Lemon or lime juice:			
Canned	1 cup	244	2
Frozen, diluted	1 cup	248	4
Orange juice: Canned	1 cup	249	5

BEVERAGES AND FRUIT JUICES

Food	Portion	Weight gms	Sodium mgs
Orange juice: cont.			
Frozen, diluted	1 cup	249	5
Tangerine juice	1 cup	249	2
Grape juice, bottled	1 cup	253	8
Peach nectar	1 cup	249	10
Pear nectar	1 cup	250	8
Pineapple juice	1 cup	250	5
Prune juice	1 cup	256	5
MINERAL WATER, IMPORTED	8 fl oz	240	42
TEA:			
Hot:			
Brewed	8 fl oz	240	1
Instant	8 fl oz	240	2
Iced:			
Canned	8 fl oz	240	9
Powdered, lemon flavored:			
Sugar sweetened	8 fl oz	240	1
Low calorie	8 fl oz	240	15
THIRST QUENCHER	8 fl oz	240	140

CONDIMENTS, FATS, AND OILS

Food	Portion	Weight gms	Sodium mgs
BAKING POWDER	1 tsp	3	339
BAKING SODA	1 tsp	3	821
CATSUP:			
Regular	1 tbsp	15	156
Low sodium	1 tbsp	15	3
CHILI POWDER	1 tsp	3	26
GARLIC:			
Powder	1 tsp	3	1
Salt	1 tsp	6	1,850
HORSERADISH, PREPARED	1 tbsp	18	198

CONDIMENTS, FATS, AND OILS

Food	Portion	Weight gms	Sodium mgs
MEAT TENDERIZER:			
Regular	1 tsp	5	1,750
Low sodium	1 tsp	5	1
MSG (MONOSODIUM GLUTAMATE)	1 tsp	5	492
MUSTARD, PREPARED	1 tsp	5	65
OLIVES:			
Green	4 olives	16	323
Ripe, mission	3 olives	15	96
ONION:			
Powder	1 tsp	2	1
Salt	1 tsp	5	1,620
PARSLEY, DRIED	1 tbsp	1	6
PEPPER, BLACK	1 tsp	2	1
PICKLES:			
Bread and butter	2 slices	15	101

Food	Portion	Weight gms	Sodium mgs
Dill	1 pickle	65	928
Sweet	1 pickle	15	128
RELISH, SWEET	1 tbsp	15	124
SALT	1 tsp	5	1,938
SAUCES:			
A-1	1 tbsp	17	275
Barbecue	1 tbsp	16	130
Chili:			
Regular	1 tbsp	17	227
Low sodium	1 tbsp	15	11
Soy	1 tbsp	18	1,029
Tabasco	1 tsp	5	24
Tartar	1 tbsp	14	182
Teriyaki	1 tbsp	18	690
Worcestershire	1 tbsp	17	206
VINEGAR	½ cup	120	1
YEAST, BAKER'S, DRY	1 package	7	1
FATS, OILS, AND RELATED PRODUCTS:			
Butter:			
Regular	1 tbsp	14	116

Food	Portion	Weight gms	Sodium mgs
Butter: continued			
Unsalted	1 tbsp	14	2
Whipped	1 tbsp	9	74
Margarine:			
Regular	1 tbsp	14	140
Unsalted	1 tbsp	14	1
Salad dressing:			
Blue cheese	1 tbsp	15	153
French:			
Home recipe	1 tbsp	14	92
Bottled	1 tbsp	14	214
Dry mix, prepared	1 tbsp	14	253
Low sodium	1 tbsp	15	3
Italian:			
Bottled	1 tbsp	15	116
Dry mix, prepared	1 tbsp	14	172
Mayonnaise	1 tbsp	15	78
Russian	1 tbsp	15	133
Thousand Island:			
Regular	1 tbsp	16	109
Low cal	1 tbsp	14	153

DAIRY PRODUCTS

Food	Portion	Weight gms	Sodium mgs
CHEESE:			
Natural:			
Blue	1 oz	28	396
Brick	1 oz	28	159
Brie	1 oz	28	178
Camembert	1 oz	28	239
Cheddar:			
Regular	1 oz	28	176
Low sodium	1 oz	28	6
Colby	1 oz	28	171
Cottage:			
Regular and lowfat	4 oz	113	457
Dry curd, unsalted	4 oz	113	14
Cream	1 oz	28	84
Edam	1 oz	28	274
Feta	1 oz	28	316
Gouda	1 oz	28	232

DAIRY PRODUCTS

Food	Portion	Weight gms	Sodium mgs
Gruyere	1 oz	28	95
Limburger	1 oz	28	227
Monterey	1 oz	28	152
Mozzarella, from:			
Whole milk	1 oz	28	106
Part skim milk	1 oz	28	132
Muenster	1 oz	28	178
Neufchatel	1 oz	28	113
Parmesan:			
Grated	1 oz	28	528
Hard	1 oz	28	454
Provolone	1 oz	28	248
Ricotta, made with:			
Whole milk	½ cup	124	104
Part skim milk	½ cup	124	155
Roquefort	1 oz	28	513
Swiss	1 oz	28	74
Tilsit	1 oz	28	213
Pasteurized processed cheese:			
American	1 oz	28	406
Low sodium	1 oz	28	2
Swiss	1 oz	28	388

DAIRY PRODUCTS

Food	Portion	Weight gms	Sodium mgs
CHEESE FOOD:			
American	1 oz	28	337
Swiss	1 oz	28	440
CHEESE SPREAD:			
American	1 oz	28	381
CREAM, SWEET:			
Fluid, all types	1 tbsp	15	6
Whipped	1 tbsp	3	4
CREAM, SOUR, CULTURED	1 tbsp	12	6
CREAM PRODUCTS, IMITATION:			
Sweet:			
Coffee whitener:			
Liquid	1 tbsp	15	12
Powdered	1 tbsp	6	12
Whipped			
topping	1 tbsp	4	2
Sour, cultured	1 oz	28	29
MILK:			
Fluid:			
Whole and			
lowfat	1 cup	244	122

Food	Portion	Weight gms	Sodium mgs
MILK: cont.			
Whole, low			
sodium	1 cup	244	6
Buttermilk,			
cultured:			
Salted	1 cup	245	257
Unsalted	1 cup	245	122
Canned:			
Evaporated:			
Whole	1 cup	252	266
Skim	1 cup	255	294
Sweetened,			
condensed	1 cup	306	389
Dry:			
Nonfat:			
Regular	½ cup	60	322
Instantized	1 cup	68	373
Buttermilk	½ cup	60	310
MILK BEVERAGES:			
Chocolate	1 cup	250	149
Cocoa, hot	1 cup	250	123
Eggnog	1 cup	254	138
Malted:			
Natural flavor	1 cup	265	215
Chocolate			
flavor	1 cup	265	168
Shakes, thick:			
Chocolate or			
vanilla	1 shake	306	317

DAIRY PRODUCTS

Food	Portion	Weight gms	Sodium mgs
MILK DESSERTS, FROZEN:			
Ice cream:			
Chocolate	1 cup	133	75
Custard, French	1 cup	133	84
Strawberry	1 cup	133	77
Vanilla:			
French,			
softserve	1 cup	173	153
Hardened	1 cup	140	112
Ice milk:			
Vanilla:			
Hardened	1 cup	131	105
Soft serve	1 cup	175	163
Novelty products:			
Bars:			
Fudge	1 bar	73	54
Orange			
cream	1 bar	66	27
Vanilla,			
chocolate			
coated:			
Ice cream	1 bar	47	24
Ice milk	1 bar	50	31
Cones, vanilla,			
chocolate			
coated	1 small	71	64
Sandwich	1 sandwich	62	92
Sherbet, orange	1 cup	193	89
MILK DESSERTS, OTHER:			
Custard, baked	1 cup	265	209

DAIRY PRODUCTS

Food	Portion	Weight gms	Sodium mgs
Puddings:			
Butterscotch:			
Regular, whole milk	½ cup	148	245
Instant, whole milk	½ cup	149	445
LoCal, skim milk	½ cup	130	130
Ready-to-serve	1 can	142	290
Chocolate:			
Home recipe	½ cup	130	73
Regular, whole milk	½ cup	148	195
Instant, whole milk	½ cup	149	470
LoCal, skim milk	½ cup	130	80
Ready-to-serve	1 can	142	262
Vanilla:			
Home recipe	½ cup	128	83
Regular, whole milk	½ cup	148	200
Instant, whole milk	½ cup	149	400
LoCal, skim milk	½ cup	130	115

DAIRY PRODUCTS

Food	Portion	Weight gms	Sodium mgs
Ready-to-serve	1 can	142	279
Tapioca, cooked	½ cup	145	130

YOGURT:			
Plain:			
Regular	8 oz	227	105
Lowfat	8 oz	227	159
Skim milk	8 oz	227	174
With fruit	8 oz	227	133

EGGS, FISH, POULTRY, AND MEATS

Food	Portion	Weight gms	Sodium mgs
EGGS:			
Whole	1 egg	50	59
White	1 white	33	50
Yolk	1 yolk	17	9
Substitute, frozen	¼ cup	60	120
FISH:			
Bass, black sea, raw	3 oz	85	57
Bluefish:			
Baked with butter	3 oz	85	87
Breaded, fried	3 oz	85	123
Bonito, canned	3 oz	85	437
Catfish, raw	3 oz	85	50
Cod, broiled with butter	3 oz	85	93
Eel, raw	3 oz	85	67

Food	Portion	Weight gms	Sodium mgs
Flounder (includes sole and other flat fish) baked with butter	3 oz	85	201
Haddock, breaded, fried	3 oz	85	150
Halibut, broiled with butter	3 oz	85	114
Herring, smoked	3 oz	85	5,234
Lingcod, raw	3 oz	85	50
Mackerel, raw	3 oz	85	40
Mullett, breaded, fried	3 oz	85	83
Ocean perch, fried	3 oz	85	128
Pollock, creamed	3 oz	85	94
Pompano, cooked	3 oz	85	48
Rockfish, oven steamed	3 oz	85	57
Salmon: Broiled with butter	3 oz	85	99
Canned: Salt added: Pink	3 oz	85	443

Food	Portion	Weight gms	Sodium mgs
Salmon: cont.			
Red	3 oz	85	329
Silver	3 oz	85	298
Without salt added	3 oz	85	41
Sardines, canned:			
Drained	3 oz	85	552
In tomato sauce	3 oz	85	338
Shad, baked with butter	3 oz	85	66
Snapper, raw	3 oz	85	56
Trout, lake, raw	3 oz	85	67
Tuna, canned:			
Light meat:			
Chunk:			
Oil pack	3 oz	85	303
Water pack	3 oz	85	288
Grated	3 oz	85	246
White meat:			
(Albacore)			
Chunk, low sodium	3 oz	85	34
Solid:			
Oil pack	3 oz	85	384
Water pack	3 oz	85	309
SHELLFISH:			
Clams, raw:			
Hard	3 oz	85	174

Food	Portion	Weight gms	Sodium mgs
Clams: cont.			
Soft	3 oz	85	30
Crab:			
Canned,			
drained	3 oz	85	425
Steamed	3 oz	85	314
Lobster, boiled	3 oz	85	212
Mussels, raw	3 oz	85	243
Oysters:			
Raw	3 oz	85	113
Fried	3 oz	85	174
Frozen	3 oz	85	323
Scallops:			
Raw	3 oz	85	217
Steamed	3 oz	85	225
Shrimp:			
Raw	3 oz	85	137
Steamed	3 oz	85	159
Canned	3 oz	85	1,955
Squid, dried	1 serving	4	183
MEAT:			
Beef:			
Cooked, lean	3 oz	85	55
Corned:			
Cooked	3 oz	85	802
Canned	3 oz	85	893
Dried, chipped	1 oz	28	1,219
Lamb, cooked,			
lean	3 oz	85	58

Food	Portion	Weight gms	Sodium mgs
Pork:			
Cured:			
Bacon:			
Cooked	2 slices	14	274
Canadian	1 slice	28	394
Ham	3 oz	85	1,114
Salt pork,			
raw	1 oz	28	399
Fresh, cooked,			
lean	3 oz	85	59
Veal, cooked,			
lean	3 oz	85	69
ORGAN MEATS:			
Brain, raw	1 oz	28	35
Gizzard, poultry,			
simmered	1 oz	28	17
Heart:			
Beef, braised	1 oz	28	29
Calf, braised	1 oz	28	32
Poultry,			
simmered	1 oz	28	14
Kidney, beef,			
braised	1 oz	28	71
Liver:			
Calf, fried	1 oz	28	33
Pork,			
simmered	1 oz	28	14

Food	Portion	Weight gms	Sodium mgs
Liver: cont.			
Poultry, simmered	1 oz	28	16
Sweetbreads, calf, cooked	1 oz	28	32
Tongue, beef, braised	1 oz	28	17
Tripe:			
Commercial	1 oz	28	13
POULTRY AND GAME:			
Chicken, roasted:			
Breast with skin	½ breast	98	69
Drumstick with skin	1 drumstick	52	47
Products:			
Canned	1 5-oz can	142	714
Frankfurter	1 frankfurter	45	617
Duck, roasted, flesh and skin	½ duck	382	227
Goose, roasted, flesh and skin	½ goose	774	543
Rabbit:			
Leg, raw	4 oz	113	40
Flesh, cooked	4 oz	113	70
Turkey, small, roasted:			
Breast with skin	½ breast	344	182

Food	Portion	Weight gms	Sodium mgs
Turkey: cont.			
Leg with skin	1 leg	245	195

SAUSAGES, LUNCHEON MEATS,
AND SPREADS:

Food	Portion	Weight gms	Sodium mgs
Beer salami, beef	1 slice	6	56
Bologna:			
Beef	1 slice	22	220
Beef and pork	1 slice	22	224
Bratwurst, cooked	1 oz	28	158
Braunschweiger	1 slice	28	324
Brotwurst	1 oz	28	315
Chicken spread	1 oz	28	115
Frankfurter	1 frankfurter	57	639
Ham:			
And cheese loaf	1 oz	28	381
Chopped	1 slice	21	288
Deviled	1 oz	28	253
Spread	1 oz	28	258
Kielbasa	1 slice	26	280
Knockwurst	1 link	68	687
Lebanon bologna	1 slice	18	228
Liver cheese	1 slice	20	245
Old fashioned loaf	1 slice	22	275

Food	Portion	Weight gms	Sodium mgs
Olive loaf	1 slice	21	312
Pepperoni	1 slice	6	122
Salami:			
Cooked:			
Beef	1 slice	22	255
Beef and pork	1 slice	22	234
Dry or hard, pork	1 slice	10	226
Sausage:			
Cooked:			
Pork	1 link	13	168
Pork and beef	1 patty	27	217
Smoked	1 link	28	264
Thuringer	1 slice	22	320
Tuna spread	1 oz	28	92
Turkey roll	1 oz	28	166
Vienna sausage	1 link	16	152

PREPARED MAIN DISHES:
Beef:
And macaroni:

Frozen	6 oz	170	673
Canned	1 cup	227	1,185
Cabbage, stuffed, frozen	8 oz	226	63
Chili con carne with beans,			

Food	Portion	Weight gms	Sodium mgs
Chili con carne: cont.			
canned:			
Regular	1 cup	255	1,194
Low sodium	1 cup	335	100
Dinners, frozen:			
Beef	1 dinner	312	998
Meat loaf	1 dinner	312	1,304
Sirloin, chopped	1 dinner	284	978
Swiss steak	1 dinner	284	682
Enchiladas	1 pkg	207	725
Goulash, canned	8 oz	227	1,032
Hash, corned beef, canned	1 cup	220	1,520
Meatballs, Swedish	8 oz	227	1,880
Peppers, stuffed, frozen	8 oz	226	1,001
Pizza, frozen:			
With pepperoni	½ pie	195	813
With sausage	½ pie	189	967
Pot pie:			
Home baked	1 pie	227	644
Frozen	1 pie	227	1,093
Ravioli, canned	7.5 oz	213	1,065

Food	Portion	Weight gms	Sodium mgs
Spaghetti, canned:			
And ground beef	7.5 oz	213	1,054
And meatballs	7.5 oz	213	942
Sauce	4 oz	114	856
Stew, canned	8 oz	227	980
Chicken:			
And dumplings, frozen	12 oz	340	1,506
And noodles, frozen	¾ cup	180	662
Chow mein, home recipe	1 cup	250	718
Dinner, frozen	1 dinner	312	1,153
Pot pie:			
Home recipe	1 pie	232	594
Frozen	1 pie	227	907
Fish and shellfish:			
Fish dinner, frozen	1 dinner	248	1,212
Shrimp:			
Dinner, frozen	1 dinner	223	758
Egg roll, frozen	1 roll	71	648

Food	Portion	Weight gms	Sodium mgs
Tuna, pot pie, frozen	1 pie	227	715
Pork, sweet and sour, canned	1 cup	275	1,968
Turkey:			
Dinner, frozen	1 dinner	333	1,228
Pot pie:			
Home recipe	1 pie	227	620
Frozen	1 pie	233	1,018
Veal Parmigiana	7.5 oz	214	1,825
Without meat:			
Chow mein, vegetable, frozen:	1 cup	240	1,273
Pizza, cheese	¼ 12-in pie	90	447
Spanish rice, canned	1 cup	221	1,370

FRUITS

Food	Portion	Weight gms	Sodium mgs
APPLES:			
Raw or baked	1 apple	138	2
Frozen, slices	1 cup	200	28
Frozen, scalloped	8 oz	227	45
Dried, sulfured	8 oz	227	210
APPLESAUCE, CANNED:			
Sweetened	1 cup	250	6
Unsweetened	1 cup	250	5
With added salt	1 cup	250	68
APRICOTS:			
Raw	3 apricots	114	1
Canned:			
Peeled	1 cup	258	27
Unpeeled	1 cup	258	10
Dried	1 cup	130	12

FRUITS

Food	Portion	Weight gms	Sodium mgs
AVOCADO, RAW	1 avocado	216	22
BANANA, RAW	1 banana	119	2
BERRIES:			
Blackberries (Boysenberries)			
Raw	1 cup	144	1
Canned	1 cup	244	3
Blueberries:			
Raw	1 cup	145	1
Canned	1 cup	250	2
Raspberries:			
Raw	1 cup	123	1
Frozen	1 package	284	3
Strawberries:			
Raw	1 cup	149	2
Frozen, sliced	1 cup	255	6
CHERRIES:			
Raw	1 cup	150	1
Frozen	8 oz	227	3
Canned	1 cup	257	10
CITRUS:			
Grapefruit:			
Raw	½ grapefruit	120	1

FRUITS

Food	Portion	Weight gms	Sodium mgs
Grapefruit: cont.			
Frozen,			
unsweetened	1 cup	244	6
Canned,			
sweetened	1 cup	254	4
Kumquat	1 kumquat	19	1
Lemon, raw	1 lemon	74	1
Oranges, raw	1 orange	131	1
Tangelo	1 tangelo	95	1
Tangerine	1 tangerine	86	1
CRANBERRY, RAW	1 cup	95	1
CRANBERRY SAUCE	1 cup	277	75
CURRANT:			
Raw	1 cup	133	3
Dried	1 cup	140	10
DATES, DRIED	10 dates	80	1
FIGS:			
Raw	1 fig	50	2
Canned	1 cup	248	3
Dried	1 fig	20	2

FRUITS

Food	Portion	Weight gms	Sodium mgs
FRUIT COCKTAIL, CANNED	1 cup	255	15
GRAPES, THOMPSON SEEDLESS	10 grapes	50	1
MANGOS, RAW	1 mango	200	1
MUSKMELON:			
Cantaloup	½ melon	272	24
Casaba	⅕ melon	230	34
Honeydew	⅕ melon	298	28
NECTARINES, RAW	1 nectarine	138	1
PAPAYA, RAW	1 papaya	303	8
PEACHES:			
Raw	1 peach	100	1
Frozen	1 cup	250	10
Canned	1 cup	256	15
Dried, uncooked	1 cup	160	10

FRUITS

Food	Portion	Weight gms	Sodium mgs
PEARS.			
Raw	1 pear	168	1
Canned	1 cup	255	15
Dried	1 cup	180	10
PINEAPPLE:			
Raw	1 cup	135	1
Canned	1 cup	255	7
PLUMS:			
Raw	1 plum	66	1
Canned	1 cup	256	10
PRUNES:			
Cooked	1 cup	213	8
Dried	5 large	43	2
RAISINS, SEEDLESS	1 cup	145	17
RHUBARB:			
Cooked, sugared	1 cup	270	5
Frozen	1 cup	270	5
WATERMELON	1/16 melon	426	8

GRAIN PRODUCTS

Food	Portion	Weight gms	Sodium mgs
BARLEY, PEARLED, COOKED	1 cup	200	6
BISCUITS, BAKING POWDER:			
Regular flour	1 biscuit	28	175
Self rising flour	1 biscuit	28	185
With milk from mix	1 biscuit	28	272
Low sodium	1 biscuit	28	1
BREAD:			
Boston brown bread	1 slice	45	120
Cornbread, homemade	1 oz	28	176
Cracked wheat	1 slice	25	148
French	1 slice	23	116

GRAIN PRODUCTS

Food	Portion	Weight gms	Sodium mgs
BREAD: cont.			
Mixed grain	1 slice	23	138
Pita	1 loaf	64	132
Rye:			
Regular	1 slice	25	139
Pumpernickel	1 slice	32	182
Salt rising	1 slice	26	66
White:			
Regular	1 slice	25	114
Thin	1 slice	16	79
Low sodium	1 slice	23	7
Whole wheat	1 slice	25	132
BREAKFAST CEREALS:			
Hot, cooked, in unsalted water:			
Corn (hominy) grits:			
Regular	1 cup	236	1
Instant	¾ cup	177	354
Cream of Wheat:			
Regular	¾ cup	184	2
Instant	¾ cup	184	5
Quick	¾ cup	184	126
Mix 'n eat	¾ cup	184	350
Farina	¾ cup	184	1
Oatmeal:			
Regular or quick	¾ cup	180	1

Food	Portion	Weight gms	Sodium mgs
Oatmeal: cont			
Instant:			
No sodium added	¾ cup	180	1
Sodium added	¾ cup	180	283
With apples and cinnamon	¾ cup	180	220
With maple and brown sugar	¾ cup	180	277
With raisins and spice	¾ cup	180	223
Ready-to-eat:			
Bran cereals:			
All-Bran	⅓ cup	28	160
Bran Chex	⅔ cup	28	262
40% Bran	⅔	28	251
100% Bran	½ cup	28	221
Raisin Brain	½ cup	28	304
Cheerios	1¼ cup	28	304
Corn cereals:			
Corn Chex	1 cup	28	297
Corn flakes:			
Low sodium	1¼ cup	28	10
Regular	1 cup	28	256
Sugar coated	¾ cup	28	274
Sugar Corn Pops	1 cup	28	105

GRAIN PRODUCTS

Food	Portion	Weight gms	Sodium mgs
Granola:			
Regular	¼ cup	34	61
No sodium			
added	¼ cup	34	16
Kix	1½ cup	28	261
Life	⅔ cup	28	146
Product 19	¾ cup	28	175
Rice cereals:			
Low sodium	1 cup	28	10
Puffed rice	2 cups	28	2
Rice Chex	1⅛ cup	28	238
Rice Krispies	1 cup	28	340
Sugar coated	⅞ cup	28	149
Special K	1¼ cup	28	265
Total	1 cup	28	359
Trix	1 cup	28	160
Wheat cereals:			
Puffed wheat	2 cups	28	2
Sugar			
coated	1 cup	28	46
Shredded			
wheat	1 biscuit	24	3
Wheat Chex	⅔ cup	28	190
Wheaties	1 cup	28	355
Wheat germ,			
toasted	¼ cup	28	1

BREAKFAST SWEETS:
Coffee cake:			
Almond	⅛ cake	42	167

GRAIN PRODUCTS

Food	Portion	Weight gms	Sodium mgs
Coffee cake: cont.			
Blueberry	⅛ cake	35	135
Honey nut	⅛ cake	55	110
Pecan	⅛ cake	40	172
Danish:			
Apple, frozen	1 roll	72	220
Cheese, frozen	1 roll	72	250
Cinnamon, frozen	1 roll	72	260
Orange, refrigerated dough	1 roll	39	329
Doughnut:			
Cake type	1 doughnut	32	160
Yeast leavened	1 doughnut	42	99
Sweet rolls:			
Apple crunch, frozen	1 roll	28	105
Caramel, frozen	1 roll	29	118
Cinnamon, frozen	1 roll	26	110
Honey	1 roll	28	119
Toaster pastry:			
Apple, frosted	1 pastry	52	324
Blueberry, frosted	1 pastry	52	242
Cinnamon, frosted	1 pastry	52	326
Strawberry	1 pastry	52	238

Food	Portion	Weight gms	Sodium mgs
CAKES, FROM MIX:			
Angel food:			
Regular	1/12 cake	56	134
One step	1/12 cake	57	250
Devils food	1/12 cake	67	402
Pound	1/12 cake	55	171
White	1/12 cake	68	238
Yellow	1/12 cake	69	242
COOKIES:			
Brownies, iced	1 brownie	32	69
Chocolate chip	2 cookies	21	69
Fig bars	2 bars	28	96
Ginger snaps	4 cookies	28	161
Macaroons	2 cookies	38	14
Oatmeal:			
Plain	1 cookie	18	77
With chocolate chips	2 cookies	26	54
With raisins	2 cookies	26	55
Sandwich type	2 cookies	20	96
Shortbread	4 cookies	30	116
Sugar	1 cookie	26	108
Sugar wafer	4 cookies	28	43
Vanilla wafer	6 cookies	24	53
CRACKERS:			
Graham	1 cracker	7	48

Food	Portion	Weight gms	Sodium mgs
CRACKERS: cont.			
Low sodium	1 cracker	4	1
Rye	1 cracker	6	70
Saltine	2 crackers	6	70
Whole wheat	1 cracker	4	30
MACARONI, COOKED	1 cup	140	2
MUFFIN, ENGLISH	1 medium	57	293
NOODLES, COOKED	1 cup	140	2
PANCAKES, FROM MIX	1 pancake	27	152
PANCAKE MIX	1 cup	141	2,036
PIES, FROZEN:			
Apple	1/8 of pie	71	208
Banana cream:	1/8 of pie	66	90
Bavarian cream:			
Chocolate	1/8 of pie	80	78
Lemon	1/8 of pie	83	71

Food	Portion	Weight gms	Sodium mgs
PIES, FROZEN: cont.			
Blueberry	⅛ of pie	71	163
Cherry	⅛ of pie	71	169
Chocolate			
cream	⅙ of pie	66	107
Coconut:			
Cream	⅙ of pie	66	104
Custard	⅛ of pie	71	194
Lemon cream	⅙ of pie	66	92
Mince	⅛ of pie	71	258
Peach	⅛ of pie	71	169
Pecan	⅛ of pie	71	241
Pumpkin	⅛ of pie	71	169
Strawberry			
cream	⅙ of pie	66	101
RICE, COOKED:			
Brown	1 cup	195	10
White:			
Regular	1 cup	205	6
Parboiled	1 cup	175	4
Quick	1 cup	165	13
ROLLS:			
Brown and			
serve	1 roll	28	138
Refrigerated			
dough	1 roll	35	342

GRAIN PRODUCTS

Food	Portion	Weight gms	Sodium mgs
SNACKS:			
Corn chips	1 oz	28	231
Popcorn:			
Caramel coated	1 cup	35	262
Oil, salt	1 cup	9	175
Plain	1 cup	6	1
Potato chips	10 chips	20	200
Pretzels:			
Regular twist	1 pretzel	6	101
Small stick	3 sticks	1	17
SPAGHETTI, COOKED	1 cup	140	2
STUFFING MIX, COOKED	1 cup	170	1,131
WAFFLE, FROZEN	1 waffle	37	275

LEGUMES AND NUTS

Food	Portion	Weight gms	Sodium mgs
ALMONDS:			
Salted, roasted	1 cup	157	311
Unsalted,			
slivered	1 cup	115	4
BEANS:			
Baked, canned:			
Boston style	1 cup	260	606
With or without			
pork	1 cup	260	928
Dry, cooked:			
Great			
Northern	1 cup	179	5
Lima	1 cup	192	4
Kidney	1 cup	182	4
Navy	1 cup	195	3
Pinto	1 cup	207	4
Kidney, canned	1 cup	255	844

LEGUMES AND NUTS

Food	Portion	Weight gms	Sodium mgs
BRAZIL NUTS, SHELLED	1 cup	140	1
CASHEWS:			
Roasted in oil	1 cup	140	21
Dry roasted, salted	1 cup	140	1,200
CHESTNUTS	1 cup	160	10
CHICKPEAS, COOKED	1 cup	169	13
FILBERTS (HAZELNUTS), CHOPPED	1 cup	115	2
LENTILS, COOKED	1 cup	188	4
PEANUTS:			
Dry roasted, salted	1 cup	144	986
Roasted, salted	1 cup	144	601

LEGUMES AND NUTS

Food	Portion	Weight gms	Sodium mgs
PEANUTS: cont.			
Spanish, salted	1 cup	144	823
Unsalted	1 cup	144	8
PEANUT BUTTER:			
Smooth or			
crunchy	1 tbsp	16	81
Low sodium	1 tbsp	16	1
PEAS:			
Blackeye,			
cooked	1 cup	204	12
Split, cooked	1 cup	237	5
PECANS	1 cup	118	1
PILINUTS	4 oz	113	3
PISTACHIOS	1 cup	125	6
SOYBEANS:			
Cooked	1 cup	180	4
Curd (tofu)	¼ block	130	9

LEGUMES AND NUTS

Food	Portion	Weight gms	Sodium mgs
SOYBEANS: cont.			
Fermented (miso):			
Red	¼ cup	72	3,708
White	¼ cup	67	2,126
WALNUTS, ENGLISH	1 cup	120	3

SOUPS

Food	Portion	Weight gms	Sodium mgs
BEEF BROTH, CUBED	1 cup	241	1,152
BEEF NOODLE:			
Condensed, with water	1 cup	244	952
Dehydrated, with water	1 cup	251	1,041
CHICKEN NOODLE:			
Condensed, with water	1 cup	241	1,107
Dehydrated, with water	1 cup	252	1,284
CHICKEN RICE:			
Condensed, with water	1 cup	241	814

Food	Portion	Weight gms	Sodium mgs
CHICKEN RICE: cont.			
Dehydrated,			
with water	1 cup	253	980
CLAM CHOWDER, MANHATTAN,			
Condensed,			
with water	1 cup	244	1,808
CLAM CHOWDER, NEW ENGLAND			
CONDENSED:			
With water	1 cup	244	914
With milk	1 cup	248	992
MINESTRONE, CONDENSED,			
With water	1 cup	241	911
MUSHROOM:			
Condensed,			
with water	1 cup	244	1,031
Condensed,			
with milk	1 cup	248	1,076
Dehydrated,			
with water	1 cup	253	1,019
Low sodium	1 cup	244	27

SOUPS

Food	Portion	Weight gms	Sodium mgs
PEA, GREEN:			
Condensed			
with water	1 cup	250	987
Dehydrated,			
with water	1 cup	271	1,220
TOMATO:			
Condensed,			
with water	1 cup	244	872
Condensed,			
with milk	1 cup	248	932
Dehydrated,			
with water	1 cup	265	943
Low sodium	1 cup	244	29
VEGETABLE:			
Condensed,			
with water	1 cup	241	823
Dehydrated,			
with water	1 cup	253	1,146
VEGETABLE BEEF:			
Condensed,			
with water	1 cup	244	957
Dehydrated,			
with water	1 cup	252	1,000
Low sodium	1 cup	244	51

SUGARS AND SWEETS

Food	Portion	Weight gms	Sodium mgs
CANDY:			
Candy corn	1 oz	28	60
Caramel	1 oz	28	74
Chocolate:			
Bitter	1 oz	28	4
Milk	1 oz	28	28
Fudge, chocolate	1 oz	28	54
Gum drops	1 oz	28	10
Hard	1 oz	28	9
Jelly beans	1 oz	28	3
Licorice	1 oz	28	28
Marshmallows	1 oz	28	11
Mints, uncoated	1 oz	28	56
Peanut brittle	1 oz	28	145
Taffy	1 oz	28	88
Toffee bar, almond	1 oz	28	65

SUGARS AND SWEETS

Food	Portion	Weight gms	Sodium mgs
JAMS AND JELLIES:			
Jam:			
Regular	1 tbsp	20	2
Low calorie	1 tbsp	20	19
Jelly:			
Regular	1 tbsp	18	3
Low calorie	1 tbsp	18	21
SYRUP			
Chocolate flavored:			
Thin	1 tbsp	19	10
Fudge	1 tbsp	19	17
Corn	1 tbsp	20	14
Maple:			
Regular	1 tbsp	20	1
Imitation	1 tbsp	20	20
Molasses:			
Light	1 tbsp	20	3
Medium	1 tbsp	20	7
Blackstrap	1 tbsp	20	18
SUGAR:			
Brown	1 cup	220	66
Granulated	1 cup	200	2
Powdered	1 cup	120	1

VEGETABLES, VEGETABLE JUICES, AND SALADS

Food	Portion	Weight gms	Sodium mgs
ARTICHOKES:			
Cooked	1 medium	120	36
Hearts, frozen	3 oz	85	40
ASPARAGUS:			
Raw	1 spear	20	1
Frozen	4 spears	60	4
Canned:			
Regular	4 spears	80	298
Low sodium	1 cup	235	7
BEANS:			
Italian:			
Frozen	3 oz	85	4
Canned	1 cup	220	913
Lima:			
Cooked	1 cup	170	2

Food	Portion	Weight gms	Sodium mgs
Lima: cont.			
Frozen	1 cup	170	128
Canned	1 cup	170	456
Low sodium	1 cup	170	7
Snap:			
Cooked	1 cup	125	5
Frozen:			
Regular	3 oz	85	3
With almonds	3 oz	85	335
With mushrooms	3 oz	85	145
With onions	3 oz	85	360
Canned:			
Regular	1 cup	130	326
Low sodium	1 cup	135	3
BEANSPROUTS, MUNG:			
Raw	1 cup	105	5
Canned	1 cup	125	71
BEETS:			
Cooked	1 cup	170	73
Canned:			
Sliced	1 cup	170	479
Low sodium	1 cup	170	110
Harvard	1 cup	170	275
Pickled	1 cup	170	330

VEGETABLES

Food	Portion	Weight gms	Sodium mgs
BEET GREENS, COOKED	1 cup	145	110
BROCCOLI:			
Raw	1 stalk	151	23
Frozen:			
Cooked	1 cup	188	35
With cheese sauce	3.3 oz	94	440
With hollandaise sauce	3.3 oz	94	115
BRUSSELS SPROUTS:			
Raw	1 medium	18	1
Frozen:			
Cooked	1 cup	150	15
In butter sauce	3.3 oz	94	421
CABBAGE:			
Green:			
Raw	1 cup	70	8
Cooked	1 cup	144	16
Red, raw	1 cup	70	18

VEGETABLES

Food	Portion	Weight gms	Sodium mgs
CARROTS:			
Raw	1 carrot	72	34
Frozen:			
Cut or whole	3.3 oz	94	43
In butter sauce	3.3 oz	94	350
With brown sugar glaze	3.3 oz	94	500
Canned:			
Regular	1 cup	155	386
Low sodium	1 cup	150	58
CAULIFLOWER:			
Raw	1 cup	115	17
Cooked	1 cup	125	13
Frozen:			
Cooked	1 cup	180	18
With cheese sauce	3 oz	85	325
CELERY, RAW	1 stalk	20	25
CHARD, COOKED	1 cup	166	143
CHICORY	1 cup	90	6

VEGETABLES

Food	Portion	Weight gms	Sodium mgs
COLLARDS:			
Cooked	1 cup	190	24
Frozen	3 oz	85	41
CORN:			
Cooked	1 ear	140	1
Frozen	1 cup	166	7
Canned:			
Cream style:			
Regular	1 cup	256	671
Low sodium	1 cup	256	5
Vacuum pack	1 cup	210	577
Whole kernel:			
Regular	1 cup	165	384
Low sodium	1 cup	166	2
CUCUMBER	7 slices	28	2
DANDELION GREENS, COOKED	1 cup	105	46
EGGPLANT, COOKED	1 cup	200	2
ENDIVE, RAW	1 cup	50	7

VEGETABLES

Food	Portion	Weight gms	Sodium mgs
KALE:			
Cooked	1 cup	110	47
Frozen	3 oz	85	13
KOHLRABI, COOKED	1 cup	165	9
LEEK	1 bulb	25	1
LETTUCE	1 cup	55	4
MUSHROOMS:			
Raw	1 cup	70	7
Canned	2 oz	56	242
MUSTARD GREENS:			
Raw	1 cup	33	11
Cooked	1 cup	140	25
Frozen	3 oz	85	25
OKRA, COOKED	10 pods	106	2
ONIONS:			
Mature, dry	1 medium	100	10

VEGETABLES

Food	Portion	Weight gms	Sodium mg's
ONIONS: cont.			
Green	2 medium	30	2
Flaked	1 tbsp	6	31
PARSLEY, RAW	1 tbsp	4	2
PARSNIPS, COOKED	1 cup	155	19
PEAS, GREEN:			
Cooked	1 cup	160	2
Frozen:			
Regular	3 oz	85	80
In butter sauce	3.3 oz	94	402
In cream sauce	2.6 oz	74	420
With mushrooms	3.3 oz	94	240
Canned:			
Regular	1 cup	170	493
Low sodium	1 cup	170	8
PEPPERS:			
Hot, raw	1 pod	28	7
Sweet, raw or cooked	1 pod	74	9

VEGETABLES

Food	Portion	Weight gms	Sodium mgs
POTATOES:			
Baked or boiled	1 medium	156	5
Frozen:			
French fried	10 strips	50	15
Salted	2.5 oz	71	270
Canned	1 cup	250	753
Instant, reconstituted	1 cup	210	485
Mashed, milk and salt	1 cup	210	632
Au gratin	1 cup	245	1,095
PUMPKIN, CANNED	1 cup	245	12
RADISH	4 small	18	2
RUTABAGA, COOKED	1 cup	200	8
SAUERKRAUT, CANNED	1 cup	235	1,554
SHALLOT	1 shallot	20	3

VEGETABLES

Food	Portion	Weight gms	Sodium mg's
SPINACH:			
Raw	1 cup	55	49
Cooked	1 cup	180	94
Frozen:			
Regular	3.3 oz	94	65
Creamed	3 oz	85	280
Canned:			
Regular	1 cup	205	910
Low sodium	1 cup	205	148
SQUASH:			
Summer:			
Cooked	1 cup	210	5
Frozen,			
with curry	⅓ cup	71	228
Canned	1 cup	210	785
Winter:			
Baked, mashed	1 cup	205	2
Frozen	1 cup	200	4
SWEET POTATOES:			
Baked or boiled			
in skin	1 potato	132	20
Canned:			
Regular	1 potato	100	48
Low sodium	1 serving	113	27
Candied	1 potato	100	42

VEGETABLES

Food	Portion	Weight gms	Sodium mgs
Yam, white, raw	1 cup	200	28
TOMATOES:			
Raw	1 tomato	123	14
Cooked	1 cup	240	10
Canned:			
Whole	1 cup	240	390
Stewed	1 cup	240	584
Low sodium	1 cup	240	16
TOMATO JUICE:			
Regular	1 cup	243	878
Low sodium	1 cup	243	9
TOMATO PASTE	1 cup	258	77
TOMATO SAUCE	1 cup	248	1,498
TURNIP GREENS, COOKED	1 cup	155	17
VEGETABLES MIXED:			
Frozen	3.3 oz	94	45
Canned	1 cup	170	380

VEGETABLES

Food	Portion	Weight gms	Sodium mgs
VEGETABLE JUICE COCKTAIL	1 cup	243	887
SALADS:			
Bean:			
Marinated	½ cup	130	104
Canned	½ cup	130	537
Carrot-raisin	½ cup	63	97
Cole slaw	½ cup	60	68
Macaroni	⅔ cup	127	676
Potato	½ cup	125	625

TABLE 2
SODIUM CONTENT OF FAST FOODS

ARBY'S

	Sodium (mg.)
Beef and Cheese	1220
Club Sandwich	1610
Ham'n Cheese	1350
Junior Roast Beef	530
Roast Beef Sandwich	880
Super Roast Beef	1420
Swiss King Sandwich	1585
Turkey Deluxe	1220
Turkey Sandwich	1060

ARTHUR TREACHER'S

	Sodium (mg.)
Chicken	240
Chicken Sandwich	454
Chips	347
Chowder	491
Cole Slaw	312
Fish	305
Fish Sandwich	491
Krunch Pup	786
Lemon Luvs	369
Shrimp	467

BURGER CHEF

	Sodium (mg.)
Big Chef	622
Cheeseburger	535
Double Cheeseburger	691
French Fries	242
Hamburger	393
Mariner Platter	882
Rancher Platter	444
Shake	167
Skipper's Treat	0.3
Super Chef	0.5

SODIUM CONTENT OF FAST FOODS

BURGER KING

	Sodium (mg.)
Cheeseburger	562
French Fries	230
Hamburger	401
Hot Dog	841
Vanilla Shake	159
Whaler	735
Whopper	909

DAIRY QUEEN

	Sodium (mg.)
Big Brazier Deluxe	920
Big Brazier Regular	910
Big Brazier W/Cheese	1435
Vanilla Shake	159
Whaler	735
Brazier W/Cheese	865
Brazier Chili Dog	939
Brazier Dog	868
Super Brazier	1619
Super Brazier Chili Dog	1640
Super Brazier Dog	1552
Super Brazier Dog W/Cheese	1986

HARDEES

	Sodium (mg.)
Big Twin	808
Cheeseburger	789
Deluxe	1063
Double Cheescburger	1251
Fish Sandwich	638
French Fries (large)	192
French Fries (small)	121
Hamburger	682
Hot Dog	744
Roast Beef Sandwich	662

KENTUCKY FRIED CHICKEN

	Sodium (mg.)
Chicken Dinner Original	2285
Chicken Dinner Extra Crispy	1915

SODIUM CONTENT OF FAST FOODS

McDONALD'S

	Sodium (mg.)
Apple Pie	414
Big Mac	962
Cheeseburger	725
Cherry Pie	456
Chocolate Shake	329
Egg McMuffin	914
English Muffin	466
Fillet O' Fish	709
French Fries	113
Hamburger	526
Hot Cakes	1071
Cookies	330
Quarter Pounder	711
Quarter Pounder W/Cheese	1209
Sausage—Pork	464
Scrambled Eggs	207
Strawberry Shake	256
Vanilla Shake	250

PONDEROSA

	Sodium (mg.)
Chopped Beef	89
Double Deluxe	99.1
Extra Cut Prime Rib	100.6
Extra Cut Ribeye	532.3
Fillet of Sole Dinner	92.8
Fillet of Sole Sandwich	46.4
Junior Patty	26.9
Prime Rib	70.6
Rib Eye	356.8
Rib Eye/Shrimp	471.2
Shrimp	182
Steakhouse Deluxe	49.8
Strip Sirloin	523.9
Super Sirloin	695.2
T-Bone	850.6
Coke	20
Coffee	2
Dr. Pepper	18.4
Milk	122
Sprite	42
Tab	30
Baked Potato	6
Butter	49
Catsup	177
Cocktail Sauce	143

PONDEROSA continued

	Sodium (mg.)
Dill Pickles	279
French Fries	4.8
Kaiser Roll	311
Mayonnaise	84
Mustard	63
Blue Cheese Salad	115

STEAK N SHAKE

	Sodium (mg.)
Baked Beans	655
Baked Ham Sandwich	1858
Chili	1156
Chili Mac	1301
Chili Three Ways	1734
Cottage Cheese	198
Egg Sandwich	490
French Fries	297
Ham/Egg Sandwich	1849
Lettuce	223
Low Calorie Platter	241
Steakburger	424
Steakburger W/Cheese	679
Triple Steakburger	468
Triple Steakburger W/Cheese	933
Toasted Cheese	606
Apple Danish	351
Apple Pie	478
Brownie	164
Cheese Cake	293
Cherry Pie	267
Chocolate Shake	177
Hot Fudge Nut Sundae	121
Ice Cream	69
Lemon Float	248

STEAK N SHAKE continued

	Sodium (mg.)
Lemon Freeze	212
Orange Float	224
Strawberry Shake	190
Vanilla Shake	181

TACO BELL

	Sodium (mg.)
Bean Burrito	272
Beef Burrito	327
Beefy Tostada	138
Bellbeefer	231
Bellbeefer W/Cheese	330
Burrito Supreme	367
Combo Burrito	300
Enchirito	1175
Pintos 'n Cheese	102
Taco	79
Tostada	101

TABLE 3
SODIUM CONTENT
OF SELECTED NON-
PRESCRIPTION DRUGS*

Product	Ingredients	Sodium content mg per dose
ANALGESIC:		
(Various)	Aspirin	49
ANTACID ANALGESIC:		
Bromo-Seltzer	Acetaminophen Sodium citrate	717
Alka-Seltzer (blue box)	Aspirin Sodium citrate	521

*Reprinted by permission from table 4 of the American Medical Association's publication "Sodium and Potassium in Foods and Drugs" that was adapted from an article by D. R. Bennett, MD, PhD, entitled "Sodium Content of Prescription and Non-Prescription Drugs." Copyright (1979) to this information is held by the AMA.

SELECTED NONPRESCRIPTION DRUGS

Product	Ingredients	Sodium content mg per dose
ANTACID LAXATIVE: Sal		
Hepatica	Sodium bicarbonate Sodium mono-hydrogen phosphate Sodium citrate	1,000
ANTACIDS:		
Rolaids	Dihydroxy aluminum Sodium carbonate	53
Soda Mint	Sodium bicarbonate	89
Alka-Seltzer Antacid (gold box)	Sodium bicarbonate Potassium bicarbonate Citric acid	276
Brioschi	Sodium bicarbonate Tartaric acid Sucrose	710
LAXATIVES: Metamucil		
Instant Mix	Psyllium Sodium bicarbonate Citric acid	250

Product	Ingredients	Sodium content mg per dose
LAXATIVES: cont.		
Fleet's		
Enema	Sodium biphosphate	250-300
	Sodium phosphate	(absorbed)
SLEEP AIDS:		
Miles Nervine		
Effer-		
vescent	Sodium citrate	544

Product	Ingredients	Sodium content mg per 100 ml
ANTACID		
SUSPENSIONS		
Milk of		
Magnesia	Magnesium hydroxide	10
Amphogel	Aluminum hydroxide	14
Basalgel	Aluminum carbonate	36
Maalox	Magnesium hydroxide Aluminum carbonate	50
Riopan	Magnesium aluminum complex	14

Product	Ingredients	Sodium content mg per 100 ml
ANTACID SUSPENSIONS: cont.		
Mylanta I	Magnesium hydroxide	76
Mylanta II	Aluminum hydroxide	160
Digel	Simethicone	170
Titralac	Calcium carbonate	220

SODIUM AND HEALTH

A
BIBLIOGRAPHY

Anderson, M.W. "Abuses of Low Sodium Content Diets in Cardiovascular Disease." *Minnesota Medicine* 35 (1952): 633–38.

Andrus, E.C. "Cardiac Diets." *Maryland State Medical Journal* 2 (1953):180–81.

Angelino, P.F. et al. "Sodium Containing and Low Salt Diet in Arterial Hypertension." *Minerva Cardioangiologica* 24 (1976):427–29.

Atkinson, S.M., Jr. "Salt, Water and Rest as a Preventative for Toxemia of Pregnancy." *Journal of Reproductive Medicine* 9 (November, 1972):223–38.

Bach, I. "Common Salt in Human Nutrition." *Orvosi Hetilap* 107 (6 December 1966):2305–07.

Bagg, E.W. *Cooking Without a Grain of Salt.* New York: Bantam, 1972.

Bakke, J. et al. "Sodium Restricted Diets for Dialysis Patients." *Hospitals* 40 (1 March 1966): 76–81.

Ball, C.O., and Meneely, G.R. "Observations on Dietary Sodium Chloride." *Journal of the American Dietetic Association* 33 (1957):366–70.

Bang, H.O. et al. "Treatment of Hypertension and Congestive Heart Failure by Sodium Chloride Poor Diet." *Acta Medica Scandinavia* supplement 239 (1950):355–58.

BIBLIOGRAPHY

Battarbee, H.D. et al. "The Toxicity of Salt." *CRC Critical Reviews in Toxicology* 5 (September, 1978):355–76.

Beevers, D.G. et al. "Salt and Blood Pressure in Scotland." *British Medical Journal* 281 (6 September 1980):641–42.

Beilin, L.J. et al. "Salt, Vascular Reactivity and Hypertension." *Clinical Science* 39 (December, 1970):p. 1-15.

Bell, T.A. et al. "Low Sodium Pickle Products for Modified Diets." *Journal of the American Dietetic Association* 60 (1972):213–17.

Berglund, G. "Can Lower Salt Intake for Everyone Decrease the Blood Pressure Problem?" *Lakartidningen* 77 (19 March 1980):1091–92.

———. "Should Salt Intake Be Cut Down to Prevent Primary Hypertension?" *Acta Medica Scandinavia* 207 (1980):241–44.

Bing, R. F. et al. "Salt Intake and Diuretic Treatment of Hypertension." *Lancet* 2 (21 July 1979):121–23.

Bisht, D.B. et al. "Studies on Threshhold of Taste for Salt with Special Reference to Hypertension." *Indiana Heart Journal* 23 (1971):137–40.

Black, D.A.K. "Salt and Hypertension." *British Journal of Nutrition* 6 (1952): 428–32.

Black, H.R. "Nonpharmacologic Therapy for Hypertension." *American Journal of Medicine* 66 (1979):837–42.

Bostad, R. et al. "Sodium Chloride Intoxication in New Born Infants." *Clinical Pediatrics* (Philadelphia) 3 (January, 1964):1–4.

Boueen, R.E. et al. "Designing Formulated Foods for the Cardiac-Concerned." *Preventive Medicine* 2 (1973):366–77.

Brainard, J.B. "Salt Load as a Trigger for Migrain." *Minnesota Medicine* 59 (1976):232–33.

Brasseur, Capart. "If We Could Speak to the Cook." *Scalpel* 114 (16 December 1961):1146–50.

Brenner, E.P. *Gourmet Cooking Without Salt.* New York: Doubleday, 1981.

Brown, W.J. et al. *Cook to Your Heart's Content: On a Low-Fat, Low-Salt Diet.* New York: Van Nostrand Reinhold, 1976.

Brunswick, J.P. et al. *How to Live Three Hundred Sixty-Five Days a Year the Salt-Free Way.* New York: Bantam, 1977.

Bullock, J. et al. "Sodium Restriction in Cardiac Failure." *Medical Journal of Australia* 1 (29 April 1972):942.

Burstyn, P. et al. "Sodium and Potassium Intake and Blood Pressure." *British Medical Journal* 281 (23 August 1980):537–39.

Burton, H.B. "Do You Use Salt?" *American Journal of Psychiatry* 128 (1971): 238–39.

Calvin, M.E. et al. "Hazards to Health. Salt Poisoning." *New England Journal of Medicine* 270 (19 March 1964): 625–26.

Campbell, H.L. "Sodium Chloride as an Adjunct to a Diet of Whole Wheat and Whole Milk." *American Journal of Physiology* 147 (1976): 340–42.

Cangiano, J.L. "Salt: A Precious Substance Which May Be Harmful." *Boletin Asociacion Medica de Puerto Rico* 73 (February, 1981):48–49.

Cantoni, M. "Adding Flavor to Sodium Restricted Diets in the Hospital." *Journal of the American Dietetic Association* 30 (1954):1146–48.

Chavez, J.F. "Iodized Salt." *American Journal of Public Health* 64 (1974):302.

Clifcorn, L.E. "Production and Consumer Aspects of Low Sodium Canned Foods." *Journal of the American Dietetic Association* 29 (1953):116–20.

Clifford, P.A. "Sodium Content of Foods." *Journal of the American Dietetic Association* 31 (1955):21–27.

BIBLIOGRAPHY

Codex Alimentaries Commission. *Recommended International Standards for Special Dietary Foods with Low Sodium Content. Including Salt Substitutes.* New York: Unipub., 1974.

Cole, S.L. "Tap Water Sodium in the Low Salt Diet." *Journal of the American Medical Association* 140 (7 May 1949): 19.

Coleman, T.G. et al. "The Role of Salt in Experimental and Human Hypertension." *American Journal of Medical Science* 264 (August 1972): 103–10.

"Comparison of Low Sodium Bacon with Regular Bacon. Clinical Study." *New York Journal of Medicine* 61 (1 October 1961):3269–70.

Connor, R.C. "Common Salt and Heart Disease." *Lancet* 1 (10 February 1968): 304.

Contreras, R.J. "Salt Taste and Disease." *American Journal of Clinical Nutrition* 31 (1978):1088–97.

Cooper, R. et al. "Correlations Between Salt Intake, Blood Pressure and Family History of Hypertension." *American Journal of Clinical Nutrition* 33 (1980):2218–20.

Corcoran, A.C. "Changing Status of Sodium Restriction in Therapy of Hypertension." *American Journal of Cardiology* 8 (1961):887–89.

Corley, W.D.,Jr. "Sodium Content of Drinking Water in Nebraska." *Nebraska Medical Journal* 50 (1965):164–66.

Cossio, P. et al. "So-Called Salt-Free Breads and Substitute Products for Table Salt." *Prensa Medica Argentina* 42 (21 October 1955):3221–23.

Currens, J.H. "Medical Treatment of Hypertensive Vascular Disease." *American Practitioner* 7 (1956):1237–41.

Dahl, L.K. "Chronic Excess Salt Consumption as an Etiologic Factor in Human Hypertension." *Heart Bulletin* 11 (July–August, 1963):61–65.

BIBLIOGRAPHY

————. "High Salt Content of Western Infants' Diet: Possible Relationship to Hypertension in the Adult." *Nature* (London) 198 (22 June 1963):1204–05.

————"Possible Role of Chronic Excess Salt Consumption in the Pathogenesis of Essential Hypertension." *American Journal of Cardiology* 8 (1961):571–75.

————"Role of Dietary Sodium in Essential Hypertension." *Journal of the American Dietetic Association* 34 (1958): 58–90.

————"Role of Genetic Factors in Susceptibility to Experimental Hypertension Due to Chronic Excess Salt Ingestion." *Nature* (London) 194 (5 May 1962):480–82.

————"Salt and Blood Pressure." *Lancet* 1 (22 March 1969):622–23.

————"Salt and Hypertension." *American Journal of Clinical Nutrition* 25 (1972); 231–44.

————"Salt in Processed Baby Foods." *American Journal of Clinical Nutrition* 21 (1968):787–92.

————"Salt Intake and Salt Need." *New England Journal of Medicine* 258 (12 June 1958):1205–08.

Dahl, L.K. et al. "Effects of Chronic Excess Salt Ingestion. Evidence That Genetic Factors Play an Important Role in Susceptibility to Experimental Hypertension." *Journal of Experimental Medicine* 115 (1 June 1962):1173–90.

————"Effects of Chronic Excess Salt Ingestion. Further Demonstration That Genetic Factors Influence the Development of Hypertension: Evidence from Experimental Hypertension Due to Cortisone and to Adrenal Regeneration." *Journal of Experimental Medicine* 122 (1 September 1965):533–45.

————"Effects of Chronic Excess Salt Ingestion. Role of Genetic Factors in DOCA-Salt and Renal

BIBLIOGRAPHY

Hypertension." *Journal of Experimental Medicine* 118 (1 October 1963):605–17.

Dahl, L.K., and Loue, R.A. "Etiological Role of Sodium Chloride Intake in Essential Hypertension in Humans." *Journal of the American Medical Association* 164 (25 May 1957):397–400.

Dana, J.B. "Clinical Implications for a Low Sodium Diet." *Journal of the Maine Medical Association* 46 (1955): 187–91.

Danowski, T.S. "Low Sodium Diets: Physiological Adaptation and Clinical Usefulness." THERAPIE PARIS 168 (6 December 1958): 1866–90.

Darby, W.J. "Why Salt? How Much?" *Medical Society of New Jersey* 77 (1980): 908–10.

De Genaro, F. et al. "Salt—A Dangerous 'Antidote'?" *Journal of Pediatrics* 78 (1971):1048–49.

Dennison, A.D., Jr. "Salt: the Cardiac's Nemesis." *Journal of the Medical Society of New Jersey* 46 (1949):139–41.

Dethier, V.G. "The Taste of Salt." *American Science* 65 (1977):744–51.

Dustan, H.R. et al. "Diuretic and Diet Treatment of Hypertension." *Archives of Internal Medicine* 133 (1974):1007– 13.

Elton, N.W. et al. "Pathology of Acute Salt Poisoning in Infants." *American Journal of Clinical Pathology* 39 (1963):252–64.

Eskwith, I.S. "The Management of Congestive Heart Failure with a Free Salt Intake." *American Journal of Cardiology* 3 (1959):184–91.

Filer, L.J., Jr. "Salt in Infant Foods." *Nutrition Review* 29 (1971):27–30.

Finberg, L. "Overt and Cryptic salt poisoning: Recognition and Prevention." *Clinical Pediatrics* (Philadelphia) 2 (1963):105–07.

Finberg, L. et al. "Mass Accidental Salt Poisoning in Infancy. A Study of a Hospital Disaster." *Journal of the American Medical Association* 184 (20 April 1963):187–90.

Finn, R. "New Evidence Linking Salt and Hypertension." *British Medical Journal* 283 (4 July 1981):57

Fishbein, M. "Salt and Blood Pressure." *Postgraduate Medicine* 45 (1969):231.

Fitzsimmons, J.T. "Thirst and Sodium Appetite." *Endeavour* 4 (1980):97–101.

Flaster, D.J. "Low Sodium Kosher Diet." *American Family Physician* 19 (May, 1979):27.

Fomon, S.J. et al. "Acceptance of Unsalted Strained Foods by Normal Infants." *Journal of Pediatrics* 76 (1970):242–46.

Fotula, M.I. "Frequency of Arterial Hypertension among Persons Using Water with an Elevated Sodium Chloride Content." *Sovetsbaia Meditsina* 30 (May, 1967):134–46.

Fourcade, J. "Diuretic or Low-Salt Diet. Can One Replace the Other?" *Nouvelle Presse Medicale* 2 (15 December 1973): 3045.

Fujita, T. et al. "Factors Influencing Blood Pressure in Salt-Sensitive Patients with Hypertension." *American Journal of Medicine* 69 (September, 1980):334–44.

Fukuchi, S. et al. "Salt Restriction Test." *Nippon Rinsho,* supplement (29 June 1979):2555–56.

Francois, B. "31 Weeks of a Regime of Diuretics and Low Salt Diets. Illustration of Several Unwanted Side Effects." *Nouvelle Presse Medicale* 3 (16 March 1974):661–64.

Freis, E.D. "Salt, Volume and the Prevention of Hypertension." *Circulation* 53 (1976):589–95.

———"Sodium in Hypertension: Clinical Aspects and Dietary Management." *Current Concepts in Nutrition* 10 (1981): 127–30.

Friedman, R. et al. "Hypertension—Salt Poisoning?" *Lancet* 2 (9 September 1978):584.

Garcia-Llaurado, J. "Low Sodium Diet: General Review." *Acta Medica Hispanica* 8 (May–June, 1950):210–23.

Garrison, G.E. "Avoiding Pitfalls in Implementing a Low Sodium Diet." *Journal of the Medical Association of Georgia* 58 (1969):58–59.

Gentle, J. "Role of Alcohol in the Aetiology of Hypertension." *Medical Journal of Australia* 1 (21 February 1981): 199.

George, C.R. et al. "Low Salt Diet and Frusemide in the Treatment of Hypertension." *Postgraduate Medicine* 56 (1980):18–22.

Gilbertson, T.J. et al. "Cooperation Between the Clinical Laboratory and the Dietician: Keeping Track of Sodium in Low Sodium Diets." *Clinical Chemistry* 27 (1981):1306.

Gillum, R.F. et al. "Changing Sodium Intake in Children. The Minneapolis Children's Blood Pressure Study." *Hypertension* 3 (1981):698–703.

Glaser, G.H. "Sodium and Seizures." *Epilepsia* 5 (1964):97–111.

Gorden, E.S. "Dietary Problems in Hypertension." *Geriatrics* 29 (1974):139– 41.

Grant, H., and Reischsman, F. "The Effects of the Ingestion of Large Amounts of Sodium Chloride on the Arterial and Venous Pressures of Normal Subjects." *American Heart Journal* 32 (1946):704–12.

Grollman, A. "The Role of Salt in Health and Disease." *American Journal of Cardiology* 8 (1961):593–602.

———. "Sodium Restriction as a Dietary Measure in Hypertension." *Journal of the American Dietetic Association* 22 (1946):864–66.

Guthrie, H.A. "Infant Feeding Practices— A Predisposing Factor in Hypertension?" *American Journal of Clinical Nutrition* 21 (1968):863–67.

BIBLIOGRAPHY

Haddy, F.J. "Mechanism, Prevention and Therapy of Sodium Dependent Hypertension." *American Journal of Medicine* 69 (1980):746–58.

Hamwi, G. et al. "Water as a Sodium Source and its Relation to Sodium Restricted Therapy Patient Response." *American Journal of Public Health* 45 (1955):1344–48.

Harrison, H.L. "Salt Restriction for the Treatment of Mild Hypertension." *Journal of the Kansas Medical Society* 80 (1979):555–58.

Haruki, H. "Common Salt and Human Life." *Naika* 12 (July, 1963):1–2.

Hau, Te-Pang. *Manufacture of Soda.* New York: American Chemical Society, 1942.

Henkin, R.I. "Salt Taste in Patients with Essential Hypertension and with Hypertension Due to Primary Hyperaldosteronism." *Journal of Chronic Diseases* 27 (1974):235–44.

Heupke, W. "Low Sodium Diet with Special Reference to Heart Disease." *Hippokrates* 28 (15 July 1957):405–08.

Heyden, S. et al. "Dietary Effects on Blood Pressure." *Nutrition and Metabolism* 24 (supplement 1, 1980):50–64.

Hill, M. "Helping the Hypertensive Patient Control Sodium Intake." *American Journal of Nursing* 79 (1979):906–09.

Hirasawa, Y. "Diet Therapy in Dialysis Treatment: Low Sodium Diet." *Japanese Journal of Clinical Medicine* 30 (1972):2537–41.

Hooper. N.L., and Sippel, E.L. "Practical Aspects of Low Sodium Diets." *Stanford Medical Bulletin* 7 (February, 1949):8–11.

Hopkins, B.E. et al. "Sodium Restriction in Cardiac Failure. A Survey of Physician Attitudes and Practices." *Medical Journal of Australia* 1 (19 February 1972):370–71.

Hyden, S. "Diet Treatment of Obese Hypertensives." *Clinical Science and Molecular Medicine* 45 (supplement 1, 1973):209s.

Irvin, B.L., and Schuck, C. "Observations of Patients on Low Sodium Diets." *Journal of the American Dietetic Association* 27 (1951):1066–70.

Isberg, E.M. "The Low Sodium Diet." *Journal of the Florida Medical Association* 35 (1948):356–61.

Isorni, P., and Benevent, J. "Limitations of Sodium Restrictions in the Treatment of Cardiac Insufficiency," *Revere du Praticein* 7 (11 July 1957):2225–26.

Ito, K. et al. "Hypertension and Salt." *Nippon Rinsho* 38 (1980):3112–19.

Jacobson, M. et al. "Dietary Sodium and the Risk of Hypertension." *New England Journal of Medicine* 303 (2 October 1980):817–18.

James, J., and Goulder, L. *The Dell Color-Coded Low-Salt Living Guide.* New York: Dell, 1980.

Jencks, T. *In Good Taste.* Berkeley: Lancaster-Miller, 1980.

Johnson, J.G. et al. "Fatal Ingestion of Table Salt by an Adult." *Western Journal of Medicine* 126 (1977):141–43.

Johnston, B., and Koh, M. *Halt No Salt: A Controlled Sodium Cookbook.* Indianapolis: Dietary Research, 1979.

Jones, E.W. et al. "Diet and Hypertension." *Practitioner* 193 (July, 1964): 50–56.

Jones, W.O. et al. "Relationship of Diet to Blood Pressure Control." *Journal of the National Medical Association* 71 (1979):1146–48

Joossens, J.V. "Mortality Rates and Dietary Fats and Salts." *Lancet 1* (1 March 1980):478–79.

Joossens, J.V. et al. "Salt Intake and Mortality

from Stroke." *New England Journal of Medicine* 300 (14 June 1979):1396.

Kaplan, N.M. "Non-Drug Treatment of Hypertension." *Australian and New Zealand Journal of Medicine* 11 (supplement, 1981):73–75.

Kare, M.R. et al. *Biological and Behavioral Aspects of Salt Intake.* New York: Academic Press, 1980.

Kaufmann, D.W. *Sodium Chloride: The Production and Properties of Salt and Brine.* New York: American Chemical Society, 1960.

Kaunitz, H. et al. "Biological Effects of Salt." *Zeitschrift fur Ernaehrungswissenschaft* 22 (supplement, 1979): 1–45.

Kent, S. "How Dietary Salt Contributes to Hypertension." *Geriatrics* 36 (June, 1981):14, 18, 20.

Kirkendall, W.M. et al. "Thiazide Diuretics and Salt Consumption in the Treatment of Hypertension." In *Systematic Effects of Antihypertension Agents,* edited by M.P. Sambhi. New York: Grune & Stratton, 1976.

Kisch, B. "Salt-Poor Diet and Jewish Dietary Laws." *Journal of the American Medical Association* 153 (19 December 1953):1472.

Kothori, M.L. et al. "Salt Free Diet for Peptic Ulcer." *Journal of the Association of Physicians* (India) 14 (1966): 221–22.

Kullman, D.A. *Low Salt Diet Guide.* Merit Publications, 1977.

Lakhanpal, R.K. "When Salt Substitutes Are Required in Low Sodium Diets." *Journal of the National Medical Association* 70 (1978):225–58.

Landowne, M. et al. "The Minimal Sodium Diet: A Controlled Study of Its Effect Upon the Blood Pressure of Ambulatory Hypertensive Subjects." *Journal of Laboratory and Clinical Medicine* 34 (1949):1380–89.

BIBLIOGRAPHY

Langford, H.G. et al. "Salt Intake and the Treatment of Hypertension." *American Heart Journal* 93 (1977):531–32.

Lauer, R.M. et al. "Blood Pressure, Salt Preference, Salt Threshhold and Relative Weight." *American Journal of Diseases of Children.* 130 (1976):493–97.

Leaf, A. et al. "Some Effects of Variation in Sodium Intake and of Different Sodium Salts in Normal Subjects." *Journal of Clinical Investigations* 28 (no. 5, part 2, 1949):1082–90.

Lee, H. "A Study on the Relationship between Essential Hypertension and Sodium Chloride." *Korean Journal of Internal Medicine* 5 (1962): 409–24.

Levin, N.A. et al. "Low Salt Diet and Cardiac Insufficiency." *Ugeskrift fur Laeger* 112 (6 April 1950):467–72.

Lindberg, B.S. "Salt, Diuretics and Pregnancy." *Gynecologic and Obstetric Investigation* 10 (1979):145–56.

Longworth, D.L. et al. "Divergent Blood Pressure Responses During Short-Term Sodium Restriction in Hypertension." *Clinical Pharmacology and Therapeutics* 27 (1980):544–46.

"Low Sodium Milk." *New England Journal of Medicine.* 268 (7 March 1963): 561.

Lowenstein, F.W. "Iodized Salt in the Prevention of Endemic Goitre: A World-Wide Survey of Present Programs." *American Journal of Public Health* 57 (1967):1815–23.

"Lowering Blood Pressure Without Drugs." *Lancet* 2 (30 August 1980): 459–61.

Luft, F.C. "Sodium Restriction in the Treatment of Hypertension." *Comprehensive Therapy* 7 (October, 1981): 15–18.

McAllister, R.C., Jr. "Chronic Salt Excess and

BIBLIOGRAPHY

Hypertension, a Cultural Epidemic." *Journal of the Tennessee Medical Association* 64 (1971): 581–83.

Macintyre, E.H. "Salt in Food." *Lancet* 2 (4 October 1980):745.

MacRae, N.M. *How to Have Your Cake and Eat It Too! Diet Cooking for the Whole Family: Diabetic, Hypoglycemia, Low Cholesterol, Low Fat, Low Salt, Low Calorie Diets.* Anchorage: Alaska Northwest, 1975.

Mahadeva, K. et al. "Salt Intake in Ceylon." *British Journal of Nutrition* 24 (1970):811–14.

Marie, J. et al. "Medical Treatment of Permanent Arterial Hypertension in Children. Critical Study of 24 Cases." *Annals of Pediatrics* (Paris) 12 (2 April 1965):251–62.

Mashaly, M. et al. "Dietary Sodium Restriction and Natriuresis in Management of Hypertension." *Journal of the Egyptian Medical Association* 57 (1974):41–48.

Matz, R. "Salt Depletion in Pregnancy." *New England Journal of Medicine* 282 (26 February 1970):514.

Mayer, J. "Clinical Nutrition." *Postgraduate Medicine* 49 (1971):193–95.

———. "Hypertension, Salt Intake and the Infant." *Postgraduate Medicine* 45 (1969):229–30.

———. "Low Sodium Diets." *Postgraduate Medicine* 49 (1971):193–95.

———. "Low Sodium Diets. Severe Restriction." *Postgraduate Medicine* 50 (1971):49–52.

Meneely, G.R. "Relation of Sodium Intake to Blood Pressure." *Transactions of the American College of Cardiology* 4 (1955):278–80.

———. "Salt." *American Journal of Medicine* 16 (1954):1–3.

BIBLIOGRAPHY

Meneely, G.R. et al. "Sodium and Potassium." *Nutrition Review* 34 (1976): 225–35.

Mhaskai, K.S. "Nutritive Value of Common Salt." *Journal of the Indian Medical Association* 17 (1948):120–27.

Michell, A.R. "Salt Appetite, Salt Intake and Hypertension: A Deviation of Perspective." *Perspectives in Biology and Medicine* 21 (1978):335–47.

Moehring, J. "Salt Loss and the Onset of Malignant Hypertension." *Journal of the Tennessee Medical Assocation* 67 (1974):920–21.

Morgan, T. et al. "Effect of Reduction in Salt Intake on Hypertension." *American Heart Journal* 97 (1979):811–12.

————."The Evidence that Salt Is an Important Alliotogical Agent, If Not the Cause of Hypertension." *Clinical Science* 57 (supplement, 1979): 459–62S.

————."Hypertension Treated by Salt Restriction." *Lancet* 1 (4 February 1978): 227–30.

Moser, M. "Sodium Restrictions. Diuretics and Potassium Loss." *Archives of Internal Medicine* 141 (1981):983–84.

Multhauf, Robert P. *Neptune's Gift: A History of Common Salt.* Baltimore: Johns Hopkins, 1978.

Nehum, L.H. "Salt and Hypertension." *Connecticut Medicine* 25 (1961): 793–95.

Nelson, C.B. et al. "The Presence of Sodium in Natural Water and Softened Hard Water in Relation to Low Sodium Diets." *Minnesota Medicine* 32 (1949): 1112.

Nelson, M. "Preparation of Low Salt Diets." *Cure Concepts of Nutrition* 10 (1981):131–42.

Newborg, B. "Sodium Restricted Diet. Sodium Content of Various Wines and Other Alcoholic Beverages." *Archives of Internal Medicine* (Chicago) 123 (1969):692–93.

BIBLIOGRAPHY

Nielson, A.L. et al. "Low Salt Diet in Treatment of Congestive Heart Failure." *British Medical Journal* 4719 (16 June 1951):1349–53.

"Nutritional Implications of Sodium Restriction." *Journal of the American Medical Association* 149 (26 July 1952): 1317.

Oliver, W.A. "The Management of Congestive Heart Failure." *Practitioner* 190 (1963):195–202.

Olmstead, E.G. et al. "Nutritional Value of Beer with Reference to the Low Salt Diet." *American Journal of Clinical Nutrition* 2 (1954):392–95.

O'Mahony, M. "Salt Taste Sensitivity: A Signal Detection Approach." *Perception* 1 (1972):459–64.

Ornstein, G.C., and Leicher, L. "Palatable Low Sodium Diet in Hypertension." *Journal of the Medical Society of New Jersey* 50 (June, 1953): 294–98.

Page, I.H., and Corcoran, A.C. "Dietary Treatment of Hypertension." *Journal of Clinical Nutrition* 1 (September–October, 1952):7–16.

Palacios Matros, J.M. "Sodium Deficient Diets." *Revista Clinica Espanola* 42 (31 July 1951): 123–27.

Papper, S. *Sodium: Its Biological Significance.* Boca Raton: CRC Press, 1981.

Parasuram, C.R. "Treatment of Congestive Cardiac Failure by a Restriction of Common Salt." *Antiseptic* 49 (1952): 288–89.

Parfry, P.S. "Sodium and Potassium Intake and Blood Pressure." *British Medical Journal* 281 (6 September 1980): 678.

Pasternick, M. "Sodium Restriction in Congestive Heart Failure." *Journal of the Tennessee Medical Association* 50 (February, 1957):49–50.

Perera, G.A. "Failure of Salt Restriction to Modify Blood Pressure in the Accelerated Phase of

Primary Hypertension." *Annals of Internal Medicine* 43 (1955):1195–98.

Perera, G.A., and Blood, B.W. "The Relationship of Sodium Chloride to Hypertension." *Journal of Clinical Investigations* 26 (1947):1109–18.

Phear, D.N. "Salt Intake and Hypertension." *British Medical Journal* 5110 (13 December 1958): 1453.

Pike, R.L. et al. "Further Evidence of Deleterious Effects Produced by Sodium Restriction During Pregnancy." *American Journal of Clinical Nutrition* 23 (1970):883–89.

Pleuss, J. et al. "Dietary Considerations in Hypertension." *Postgraduate Medicine* 69 (June, 1981):34–43.

Plolz, M. "The Salt-Poor Diet." *New York State Journal of Medicine* 49 (15 June 1949):1439.

Postnov-Iu, V. "Role of Salt Regime in the Development of Arterial Hypertension." *Kardiologica* 12 (July, 1972): 5–12.

"Potassium in Salt Substitutes." *New England Journal of Medicine* 292 (15 May 1975):1082.

Puyau, F.A. et al. "Infant Feeding Practices, 1966. Salt Content of the Modern Diet." *American Journal of Disease of Children* III (1966):370–73.

Ram, C.V. et al. 'Moderate Sodium Restriction and Various Diuretics in the Treatment of Hypertension." *Archives of Internal Medicine* 141 (1981):1015–19.

Reimer, A. "Planning a Low Sodium Diet." *Public Health Nursing* 43 (1951): 496–98.

———. "Sodium Restricted Diets, a Bookshelf." *Journal of the American Dietetic Association* 33 (February, 1957): 104–07.

Richman, S. et al. "Providing a 'Brown Bag' Lunch for Ambulatory Hemodialysis Patients." *Jour-*

nal of the American Dietetic Association 70 (1977): 394–96.

Robertson, J.L. "Salt Intake and the Pathogenesis and Treatment of Hypertension." *Clinical Science* 57 (supplement 5, December, 1979): 453s–54s.

Robinson, C.H. "Planning the Sodium Restricted Diet." *Journal of the American Dietetic Association* 31 (1955): 28–33.

———. "The Sodium Restricted Diet." *American Journal of Clinical Nutrition* 3 (1955):339–43.

Robinson, M. "Salt in Pregnancy." *Lancet* 1 (25 January 1958):178–81.

"The Role of Salt in the Fall of Blood Pressure Accompanying Reduction in Obesity." *New England Journal of Medicine* 258 (12 June 1958): 1186–92.

Roth, J. *Salt-Free Cooking with Herbs and Spices.* Chicago: Contemporary Books, 1977.

Row, D.J. "Salt and Sugar in the Diet." *Canadian Medical Association Journal* 119 (7 October 1978):786–90.

"Salt in the Infant's Diet." *Nutrition Review* 25 (1967):82–84.

"Salt, Palatability and Future Health." *Medical Journal of Australia* 1 (30 May 1970):1081–82.

"Salt Restriction to Prevent Hypertension." *Medical Letter on Drugs and Therapeutics* 22 (8 February 1980):14–16.

Saunders, E. "Dietary Salt (NaCl) Intake and Arterial Hypertension." *Maryland State Medical Journal* 19 (1970):103–04.

———. "Dietary Salt (NaCl) Intake and Arterial Hypertension." *Maryland State Medical Journal* 19 (1971):109–110.

Sasaki, N. "High Blood Pressure and the Salt

Intake of the Japanese." *Japanese Heart Journal* 3 (1962):313–24.

———. "The Relationship of Salt Intake to Hypertension in the Japanese." *Geriatrics* 19 (1964):735–44.

Schechter, P.J. et al. "Salt Preference in Patients with Untreated and Treated Essential Hypertension." *American Journal of Medical Science* 267 (1974): 320–26.

———. "Sodium Chloride Preference in Essential Hypertension." *Journal of the American Medical Association* 225 (10 September 1973):1311–15.

Schlierf, G. et al. "Salt and Hypertension: Data from the 'Heidelberg Study.' " *American Journal of Clinical Nutrition* 33 (1980):872–75.

Schroeder, H.A. et al. "Low Sodium Chloride Diets in Hypertension: Effects on Blood Pressure." *Journal of the American Medical Association* 140 (4 June 1949):458–63.

Schwartz, W.K. "Saltwater Intoxication." *Journal of the American Medical Association* 240 (22 September 1978): 1338–39.

Scott, E.P. and Rotondo, C.C. "Salt Intoxication: Accidental Ingestion of a Large Amount of Sodium Chloride. Report of a Case with Autopsy of a Two Year Old Infant."*Kentucky Medical Journal* 45 (1947):107–09.

Searright, M. "A Low Sodium Potluck Luncheon." *Nursing Outlook* 16 (August, 1968):30–32.

Simmonds, R. "Food in Hospital: Basic and Special Diets." *Lancet* 1 (18 June 1949):1061–63.

Simpson, F.O. "Salt and Hypertension: A Sceptical Review of the Evidence." *Clinical Science* 57 (supplement 5, 1957):463s–80s.

Sinar, L.J. et al. "Sodium in Four Canned Vegetables. Effect on Rising and Heating in Water."

Journal of the American Dietetic Association 66 (1975): 155–57.

Skinner, E.P. "Practical Dietetics. Low Salt Diets." *Practitioner* (London) 48 (1 January 1959): 115–21.

Skrabal, F. et al. "Low Sodium/High Potassium Diet for Prevention of Hypertension: Probable Mechanisms of Action." *Lancet* 2 (24 October 1981):895– 900.

Snively, W.D., Jr. et al. "Sodium Restricted Diet: Review and Current Status." *Nursing Forum* 13 (1974):59–86.

――――. "The Sodium Restricted Diet Revisited." *Journal of the Indiana State Medical Association* 67 (1974):1067–76.

Snyder, E.L. et al. "Abuse of Salt 'Substitutes.' " *New England Journal of Medicine* 292 (6 February 1975):320.

Soda-Quiroza, E. "Rest and Diet in Cardiac Insufficiency." *Gaceta Medica de Mexico* 92 (1962): 15–18.

Sodi-Pallares, D. et al. "The Principal Etiological Factors of Coronary Disease. A New Metabolic Concept." *Archives del Instituto de Cardiologica de Mexico* 44 (September–October, 1974):689–96.

"Sodium Chloride Intake and Occurence of Hypertension. *Nutrition Review* 13 (1955): 79, 81.

"Sodium Restricted Diets: The Rationale, Complications and Practical Aspects of their Use." *Journal of the American Medical Association* 156 (13 November 1954): 1081–83.

"Sodium Restriction and Thiazide Diuretics in the Treatment of Hypertension." *Medical Journal of Australia* 1 (28 June 1975):803–07.

"Sodium Restriction in Hypertension." *Nutrition Review* 10 (1952):5–6.

BIBLIOGRAPHY

Soloff, L.A. and Zatuchni, J. "Syndrome of Salt Depletion Induced by a Regimen of Sodium Restriction and Sodium Diuresis." *Journal of the American Medical Association* 139 (16 April 1949):1136–39.

Sooch, S.S. et al. "Prevention of Endemic Goitre with Iodized Salt." *Bulletin of the World Health Organization* 49 (1973): 307–12.

Spinella, J.R. "The Problem of Restricted Dietaries with Special Reference to Low Sodium Diets." Medical Nutrition Laboratory—U.S. Army Project No. 6-60-11-017 Report No. 107:1-61, May 22, 1953.

"Surprising Observation on Relationship Between Salt and Hypertension." *Public Health Report* 93 (1978):680.

Suwanik, R. "Endemic Goitre and Experiences with Iodated Salt in the Control of Goitre in Phrae Province, Thailand." *Journal of the Medical Association of Thailand* 62 (supplement 2, 1979): 23–37.

Swales, J.D. "Dietary Salt and Hypertension." *Lancet* 1 (31 May 1980): 1177–79.

Swaye, P.S. et al. "Dietary Salt and Essential Hypertension." *American Journal of Cardiology* 29 (1972): 33–38.

Talbott, J.H. "Use of Lithium Salts and Substitutes for NaCl." *Archives of Internal Medicine* 85 (1950): 1–10.

Talso, P.J. "The Low Salt Syndrome in Congestive Heart Failure: the Importance of Dietary Sodium Restriction." *Illinois Medical Journal* 115 (1959): 348–49.

Thorburn, A.H., and Turner, P. *Living Salt Free . . . And Easy*. New York: New American Library, 1976.

Thoreson, P.A. "Planning Low Sodium Meals: A

Community Project." *New England Journal of Medicine* 246 (15 May 1952): 771–74.

Thulin, T. et al. "Salt and Blood Pressure in Scotland." *British Medical Journal* 281 (11 October 1980): 1005.

Thurston, H. et al. "Influence of Sodium Restriction Upon Two Models of Renal Hypertension." *Clinical Science and Molecular Medicine* 51 (1976): 275–79.

Tobian, L. "The Relationship of Salt to Hypertension." *American Journal of Clinical Nutrition* 32 (supplement 12, December, 1979):2739–48.

———. "Salt and Hypertension." *Annals of the New York Academy of Science* 304 (30 March 1978):178–202.

———. "Salt and Hypertension." *Journal of the Medical Association of Georgia* 69 (1980):827–34.

———. "Salt (NaCl) and Hypertension: Pathogenic Considerations." *Current Concepts in Nutrition* 10 (1981):101–11.

Tremolieres, J. "Low Sodium Diets: Physiology, Indications and Application." *Therapie Paris* 8 (1953):499–527.

Trocme, C. "Diet and Drugs in Arterial Hypertension." *Nouvelle Presse Medicale* 3 (12 January 1974):91.

———. "Seventy Years of the Salt-Free Diet." *Novelle Presse Medicale* 2 (14 July 1973): 1911.

Trowell, H. "Sodium and Potassium Intake and Blood Pressure." *British Medical Journal* 281 (13 September 1980): 744.

Tuthill, R.W. et al. "Drinking Water Sodium and Blood Pressure in Children: A Second Look." *American Journal of Public Health* 71 (1981): 722–29.

Vaidya, A.B. et al. "Common Salt and the Common Cold." *Lancet* 1 (19 June 1965): 1329–30.

Vaidya, S.K. et al. "Treatment of Congestive Cardiac Failure: A New Approach." *Indiana Journal of Medical Science* 18 (1964):88–98.

Verdonk, G. "Salt Restriction in Hypertension." *Lancet* 2 (27 September 1980): 703.

Vogl, A. "The Low Salt Syndrome in Congestive Heart Failure." *American Journal of Cardiology* 3 (1959):192–98.

Wacker, W.E. et al. "Bananas as Low Sodium Dietary Staple." *New England Journal of Medicine* 259 (6 November 1958):901–04.

Walker, S.H. et al. "Sodium and Water Content of Feedings for Use in Infants with Diarrhea." *Clinical Pediatrics* (Philadelphia) 20 (1981): 199–204.

Warmington, H.S. "The Normal Diet." *Modern Hospital* 77 (October, 1951): 110–16.

Warren, S.E. et al. "Sympathetic Nervous System Activity During Sodium Restriction in Essential Hypertension." *Clinical Cardiology* 3 (1980):348–51.

Weigel, H. "Dietetic and Medical Treatment of Hypertension." *Hippokrates* 33 (15 May 1962): 393–95.

Weiner, B. et al. "Salt Substitute as a Potassium Supplement." *American Journal of Hospital Pharmacology* 36 (1979): 446.

Weinsier, R.L. "Salt and the Development of Essential Hypertension." *Preventive Medicine* 5 (March, 1976):7–14.

Weller, J.M., and Hoobler, S.W. "Salt Metabolism in Hypertension." *Annals of Internal Medicine* 50 (1959):106–14.

Wertheim, A.R. "The Role of Diet in the Treatment of Primary Hypertension." *Transactions of the American College of Cardiology* 5 (December, 1955): 89–95.

Whitelaw, A.G. et al. "Hypertension, Edema and Suppressed Renin Aldosterone System Due to Unsupervised Salt Administration." *Archives of Diseases of Children* 50 (1975):400–01.

Whittlesey, M. *Killer Salt.* New York: Avon, 1978.

Wigand, H. "Clinical Results with Sodium Free Kreuznacher Diet Salt." *Therapei der Gegnwart* (Berlin) 94 (1955):417–18.

Wilhelmsen, L. "Salt and Hypertension." *Clinical Science* 57 (supplement 5, December, 1979): 455s–58s.

Wilkins, G.N. "The Patient, the Nurse and the Low Sodium Diet." *American Journal of Nursing* 53 (1953):445–46.

Willett, W.C. "Drinking-Water Sodium and Blood Pressure: A Cautious View of the 'Second Look.' " *American Journal of Public Health* 71 (1981): 729–32.

Winer, B.M. "Salt Metabolism in Hypertension." *Angiology* 14 (February, 1963):69–73.

Wojta, M.C. "Increasing the Appeal of the Low-Sodium Diet." *Hospitals* 37 (1 February 1963): 73–76.

Wolf, A.V. et al. "The Relative Importance of Dietary Sodium Chloride and Water in Cadiac Edema." *Federation Proceedings* 6 (no. 1, part 2, 1947):229.

Young, L.G. "Death Due to Aspiration of Table Salt." *New Zealand Medical Journal* 65 (1966): 615–16.

Youngstrom, K.A. "Low Sodium Diet. A Personal Experience of its Benefits and Pleasures." *Journal of the Kansas Medical Society* 72 (1971): 263–64.

Zarling, E.J. et al. "Bezoar Therapy. Complications Using Adolph's Meat Tenderizer and Alternatives from Literature Review." *Archives of Internal Medicine* 141 (1981):1699–770.

Zham'lanova, D.T. "Interrelationships Between the Excess Consumption of Table Salt and Arterial Pressure." *Sovetsbaia Meditsina* 5 (1981):20–23.

ABOUT THE AUTHOR

Kermit Tantum received his M.D. at Temple University and his residency in Anesthesia at the University of Pennsylvania Hospital in Philadelphia. He taught anesthesiology at the University of Pennsylvania's School of Medicine before becoming the Medical Director of both the Intensive Care Units and the Division of Respiratory Therapy at the Milton S. Hershey Medical Center at the Pennsylvania State University. In addition to his directorial responsibilities at the Hershey Medical Center, he is its Chief of the Division of Respiratory and Intensive Care in the Department of Anesthesia, and he serves as Chairman of the Center's Special Units and Critical Complex Task Force Committees. He has also been widely published in many medical and scientific journals and anthologies, including *The New England Journal of Medicine*.

Dr. Tantum currently practices medicine in Pennsylvania, where he lives with his wife and three children.